The Experiential Student Team Consulting Process

A Problem-Based Model For Consulting and Service-Learning

Ronald G. Cook | Paul Belliveau | Diane K. Campbell

CENGAGE
Learning·

Australia • Brazil • Japan • Korea • Mexico • Singapore • Spain • United Kingdom • United States

The Experiential Student Team Consulting Process: A Problem-Based Model For Consulting and Service-Learning
Ronald G. Cook | Paul Belliveau | Diane K. Campbell

Executive Editors:
 Maureen Staudt
 Michael Stranz

Senior Project Development Manager:
 Linda deStefano

Marketing Specialist:
 Courtney Sheldon

Senior Production/Manufacturing Manager:
 Donna M. Brown

Production Editorial Manager:
 Kim Fry

Sr. Rights Acquisition Account Manager:
 Todd Osborne

For product information and technology assistance, contact us at
Cengage Learning Customer & Sales Support, 1-800-354-9706

For permission to use material from this text or product,
submit all requests online at **cengage.com/permissions**
Further permissions questions can be emailed to
permissionrequest@cengage.com

Compilation © 2012 Cengage Learning

ISBN-13: 978-1-285-11542-9

ISBN-10: 1-285-11542-2

Cengage Learning
5191 Natorp Boulevard
Mason, Ohio 45040
USA

Cengage Learning is a leading provider of customized learning solutions with office locations around the globe, including Singapore, the United Kingdom, Australia, Mexico, Brazil, and Japan. Locate your local office at:
international.cengage.com/region.

Cengage Learning products are represented in Canada by Nelson Education, Ltd.

For your lifelong learning solutions, visit **custom.cengage.com.**

Visit our corporate website at **cengage.com.**

Printed in the United States of America

ABOUT THE AUTHORS

Ron Cook is a Professor, and the Entrepreneurial Studies Program Director at Rider University, where he develops and teaches upper-level undergraduate and MBA courses in team-based small business consulting, entrepreneurship/small business, new venture planning and corporate entrepreneurship. He directs Rider's Center for Entrepreneurial Studies and heads Rider's Small Business Institute®, where his student consulting teams have earned multiple national and regional awards for excellence. Ron is a member, a Fellow, a Mentor, and past president of the Small Business Institute® association. He has published a number of award-winning articles on small business and entrepreneurship and was the recipient of Rider University's Distinguished Teaching Award. He serves on the Editorial Board of the *Journal of Small Business and Enterprise Development* and is also a member of the United States Association for Small Business and Entrepreneurship,

Paul Belliveau is Principal of Paul Belliveau Associates, which provides strategic business planning and new product development counsel to small businesses. He is also an Adjunct Professor of Entrepreneurial Studies, Rider University, and served as full-time Director of the MBA Team Consulting Program, Rutgers Business School, Rutgers University. His student consulting teams from both institutions have won awards. Paul is a member and former President of the Product Development and Management Association (PDMA), and is Co-Editor of the PDMA toolbook series on new product development. He has published a number of articles on experiential student team consulting, small business and entrepreneurship. Paul is currently Associate Editor of *The Journal of Small Business Strategy* and serves on the Editorial Board of *The Small Business Institute Journal*. He is a member and former Vice President of the Small Business Institute® and belongs to the United States Association for Small Business and Entrepreneurship.

Diane K. Campbell, Associate Professor-Librarian, is a Business and Instruction Librarian at Rider University. She serves as a liaison to the College of Business Administration and as the Research Instruction Program Co-Coordinator. She has a Master's in Business Administration from Rider University and a Masters' in Library and Information Science from the School of Communication & Information at Rutgers University. Diane supports Rider's Entrepreneurial Studies program and collaborates with classroom faculty in course design to improve learning outcomes. She has co-published with entrepreneurial studies faculty. She belongs to the Small Business Institute®, and is Member-at-Large on the Executive Committee of the Business Reference and Services Section of the American Library Association.

TABLE OF CONTENTS

Preface

Welcome to the fourth edition of *The Experiential Student Team Consulting Process.*

Ron Cook, Paul Belliveau and Diane Campbell are experts in this emerging field of multi-disciplined learning. Experiential learning often takes place in capstone courses and requires instructors to take a clinical rather than classroom approach. We share a passion for the process and the desire to contribute to the improvement of the student, client and instructor experiences. By sharing our best practices in these pages, we provide you with in-depth, how-to knowledge, and a number of examples, tools, and templates that you can readily use throughout your own experiential consulting process. This book should be most helpful in meeting the integrative demands of your experiential learning.

We describe our experiential process in Chapter One. After describing the Conceptual Framework in Chapter Two, Chapters Three through Six are devoted to the four phases in our Process Flow Model: Initiation, Client, Project, and Outcomes. Chapter Seven describes how the Student Team Consulting Process is an excellent fit for Service-Learning environments. Chapter Eight describes an Assurance of Learning Model that is appropriate for experiential team consulting classes. The Appendices contain more than a dozen examples, tools and templates for your use.

New in this edition: We offer four major additions to further help students and instructors cope with the intricacies of this kind of learning, and demonstrate that learning has occurred.

- The first is to use problem-based learning theory as the framework for experiential learning as applied to student team consulting and service-learning.
- The second is to apply our proven approach in the student team consulting model to problems inherent in service-learning projects.
- The third is enhancements to the Assurance of Learning Model for experiential team-based courses. This model can meet AACSB requirements for demonstrating that individual student learning has occurred in a team-based environment.
- The fourth is substantial upgrades to our appendices including a new final consulting report, its final presentation, and a restructuring of the appendices into three sections of tools, templates, and examples. You will also find other improvements and updates throughout the appendices.

We also need to acknowledge and thank two individuals for their contribution to this edition. First is Kerry Peluso. Kerry is an Associate Vice President for Research Administration at Emory University, with expertise in experiential learning and assurance of learning. Her knowledge and research helped create the Assurance of Learning model that premiered in the third edition. The second is Lou Cooperhouse, President and CEO of Food Spectrum, LLC and of Spectrum Growth Holdings, LLC. Lou was the faculty advisor on the "Grains for Good" consulting project, and prepared the final report found in Appendix 3B. We also want to thank the general manager of Spruce Industries, Dan Josephs. Spruce was the client for the "Feasibility Study on Entering the Consumer Market for "Green" Cleaning Products" consulting project, also in Appendix 3B. Our heartfelt thanks to all of them for their contributions.

This book is written to help students by providing conceptual and practical process models that they can adapt for use in their own projects. Clients should find it helpful in maximizing their results. We share our best practices with instructors to offer a pedagogically sound, integrative approach to experiential learning. Enjoy!

Ron Cook
Paul Belliveau
Diane Campbell

Chapter One - Introduction

This chapter introduces the textbook and how it can be used by students and instructors while working with their clients. The text is the accumulation of best practices in student team consulting gained from directing thousands of students who have worked on hundreds of projects. Teams using our models have won numerous awards.

Students are the primary audience for this text. The textbook first explains the consulting process, and then depicts it in a chronological flow. Students should read the entire text as they begin a consulting assignment. Once teams are formed and the consulting process is underway, students should revisit each section as needed. Further, students are encouraged to examine the appendices closely. The appendices provide an invaluable resource as they include examples, tools and templates for student use.

Instructors can use this text in a similar fashion. By requiring their students to read the entire book before students begin a consulting assignment, instructors can remind students to refer to the appropriate chapter(s) as the process unfolds. Additionally, instructors can utilize the examples in the appendix to help structure their course.

Instructors should also provide a copy of the text to each client involved in their program, and request that the client read it prior to the consulting engagement. When a client signs up for a student consulting program, they may not understand the difference between a student consulting team and a professional consultant, or they might consider the experiential student team consulting process similar to an internship. Clients should understand this process, their responsibilities as clients, and how they can help enhance the students' learning experience.

Experiential student team consulting, referred to in this text as STC, is one of the best learning tools for college students. The practical knowledge and experience gained by participating in these programs is unmatched in higher education. Because it involves three parties operating in a real world environment, there is learning not found in a classroom-based course. This textbook is designed to help facilitate that learning.

Chapter Two – The Process of Experiential Student Team Consulting

In this chapter, you will find a definition of experiential student team consulting, a discussion of the importance of experiential learning, a conceptual framework, the purpose of fieldwork, and considerations of confidentiality and ethics.

<u>Definition</u>

Student team consulting has become an invaluable experiential learning program for undergraduate and graduate business students at or near the completion of their academic careers. In 1971, Rutgers University established one of the first programs of its kind in the United States, the Rutgers MBA Team Consulting Program.[i] In 1972, the Small Business Institute® program (SBI) began as a cooperative venture between colleges and universities and the U.S. Small Business Administration. At its peak, fieldwork, as it was commonly called, grew to encompass over 400 schools.[ii] Rutgers and an increasing number of other institutions continue to provide similar offerings of experiential student team consulting as a multi-discipline, capstone course. These programs, some required, others elective, allow students to integrate their academic and life experiences in a problem-solving or consulting endeavor with real clients who can benefit from the solutions developed.

Fieldwork is faculty-guided, experiential student consulting. What is meant by that? In part, this process can be explained by telling what it is not. It is not an internship where a student works under someone's direct supervision for "x" hours a week, for academic credit, and perhaps pay. It is not a hypothetical project or case that is conducted only in class. Fieldwork involves an actual client and a real situation. It can best be described by picturing a company hiring an outside consultant. When a consultant begins to work with a client, all of the needed information may not be available, and what is available can be inaccurate. Student team consulting places students in real-world situations where they address real-world needs.[iii]

<u>Experiential Learning</u>

Experiential learning is a broad category that encompasses a range of learning activities from internships to consulting projects to student-run ventures. It is considered more holistic than classroom-only instruction and helps bridge the gap between what the students learn passively and the actual job expectations that students encounter when they enter the working world. [iv]

This text is about experiential learning through student team consulting and gaining knowledge, and demonstrates how the consulting process enhances student learning. As stated by Kickul, Griffiths and Bacq (p. 654):

> ...to gain genuine knowledge from an experience, certain abilities are required:
> - the learner must be willing to be actively involved in the experience;
> - the learner must possess and use analytical skills to conceptualize the

experience;
- the learner must possess decision-making and problem-solving skills to
use the new ideas gained from the experience; and,
- the learner must be able to reflect on the experience. [v]

Specifically, the methodology used in experiential student team consulting is called problem-based learning (PBL).[vi] What better way to prepare students for the "real world" that to have them engaged in a consulting process? As noted by Peterson, when discussing PBL (p. 632):

> ...in the workplace, problems are ill structured, ambiguous, messy, complex, and most often do not have one correct answer that can be found at the end of the book in the answer key.... These types of problems provide a powerful learning opportunity.... This new learning paradigm also makes the learning process messy.... No longer is the path to success clear. This paradigm requires that the students first identify what the real problem is, next identify what they know and need to know, and then identify viable solutions through both creative and critical thinking.[vii]

Further, in consulting projects, students often discover that their client's business decisions are not always made on a rational basis and instead, find an emotional justification. As a result, PBL projects also offer the possibility of "eureka" moments, where students learn about less-than-ideal business decision making.[viii]

Therefore, part of the consulting process is learning how to manage ambiguity. In conducting fieldwork, the students operate under this type of uncertainty. Since fieldwork involves an actual client and a real-life experience, the situation will also be fluid and information may change over the course of the consulting assignment. Therefore, as noted in the above explanation of PBL, fieldwork requires an integrated, holistic approach that examines the issues from different business perspectives, as well as from different functional disciplines. Students learn that there can be multiple solutions, and understand when to change their mindset from one of inquiry, i.e., questioning the pros and cons of multiple approaches, to one of advocacy, i.e., deciding to pursue one approach and then making a strong case for that choice.

PBL methodology allows students to research unstructured, complex problems. These types of problems require the students to define the issues, develop alternative solutions, and pick an option.[ix]

The student team consulting model also shares some similarities with service-learning pedagogy, as both "seek to balance academic rigor with a practical relevance which furnishes students with a broader and, we argue, richer, educational experience."[x] They address one of the most salient criticisms of business education today - the absence of realistic experience, applied learning, and grounded personal development.[xi]

Fieldwork is thus an excellent mechanism to improve research abilities and critical thinking skills. As Brownell and Jamison state (p. 654):

> Fieldwork provides an interdisciplinary catalyst to motivate students' cognitive and affective learning but also as an impetus for skills-oriented learning by providing team tasks that interweave challenges from several disciplines. A well-chosen problem yields a group of team tasks that requires integrated learning rather than fragmented learning. An interdisciplinary approach is realistic because business problems usually cut across typical curricular boundaries. Thus, PBL encourages students to develop implementation skills that mirror those required to meet future challenges that they will face.[xii]

Students will be challenged to not only discover information about a particular issue but in many cases, they need to determine if this issue is important at all. In one student's words: "Unlike a regular course where we are told to read chapter 6 and answer questions 1-5, the consulting experience required us to consider whether chapter 6 even mattered and if so, which questions were important. More than anything else, we learned to ask good questions." Because of this inherent need to ask good questions, students' research included synthesizing materials from a wide variety of sources. Therefore, through the learning techniques utilized in the student consulting process, students learned important business concepts, how companies functioned, and how methods of inquiry help clarify complex business situations.[xiii]

The educational process is much more than memorizing a set of facts and figures. It is about lifelong learning, and equipping the student with the skills to handle ambiguous situations. Fieldwork does just that.

Fieldwork projects can vary based on the time and complexity of the consulting assignment, and whether these projects are part of other classes or are a separate course. Regardless of their structure, all projects involve a client, an instructor, and students, both individually and as a team.

Conceptual Framework

The experiential student team consulting model has four constituencies: the client, the student team, the student, and the instructor. These are depicted as the four circles C, T, S, and I in the model (see Figure 1). This model represents all the players in an experiential student team consulting environment.

Figure 1- Experiential Student Team Consulting Model

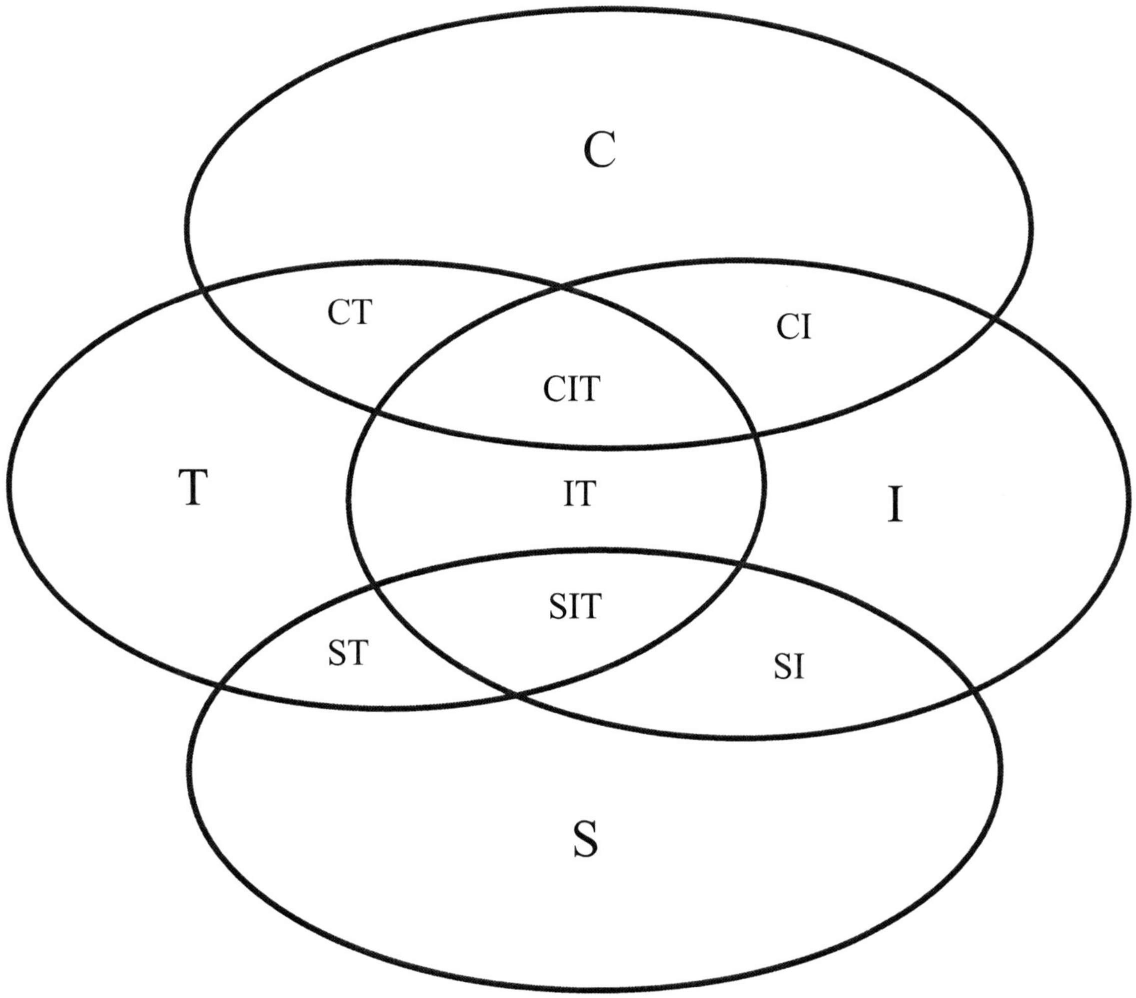

Key:

C = Client
T = Team
S = Student
I = Instructor

The client (C) represents the firm/organization who will be the beneficiary of the consulting engagement. Depending on the size of the firm, the client can be more than one person (or single point of contact) but under most consulting assignments, there is usually one point person. The client typically works initially with the instructor, then with the team and finally with the team and the instructor to wrap up the engagement.

The circle S represents the student consultant as an individual involved in the consulting process. The student works within the team (T). The team interacts with the client, the instructor, and among its individual members. In viewing the model, the individual student (S) and the client never interact. Under this consulting framework, the team is considered the consulting professional and the viewpoints expressed to the client by the team's contact person (the team leader) represents the team's position, and are not the opinion of the individual student.

The instructor (I) has the opening role in the process as s/he coordinates with the client initially, and sets up the student team. S/he later facilitates the team during the consulting engagement, interacts with each student individually, and concludes the consulting course. Student interactions with the instructor begin when the consulting assignments are being structured, during any points in the engagement where individual grading occurs, and if problems arise. The time constraints of the academic calendar will help determine how proactive the instructor needs to be regarding problem solving.

The next focus is on the model's multiple interactions, which provide an understanding of how the consulting process works. There are seven interactions, represented by overlapping circles in the model. The team and the instructor have a greater role, as measured by the number of possible interactions, at five each. The client and the student each have three interaction possibilities.

The area CT represents the client and team interactions. These interactions occur during the regular course of a consulting engagement and are both formal and informal. Formal interactions would be activities as site visits to the client, client progress reports, and the final presentation. An informal interaction could be an information request to the client. The area CI represents the client and instructor interaction to set up the consulting engagement, prior to the project beginning, and then at the end of the assignment when the client is asked to evaluate the quality of the team's work. During the consulting engagement, the client and the instructor would not usually interact. The instructor is more of a behind-the-scenes facilitator or coach for the team. The area CIT is where the client, instructor, and team all interact. Some engagements may have interim formal reports to the client, and all engagements will have a formal presentation to the client done at the end of the project. In addition, CIT interactions can also occur informally as a troubleshooting mechanism, when there is a problem with the team and the client which requires the instructor to bring all parties together.

The highest frequency of interactions usually occurs in the area IT, the core of experiential learning. This is because of the nature of the student team consulting model. The team will be in regular communication with the instructor, both reporting on the progress of the consulting engagement and receiving guidance on how to be consultants. The frequency will vary depending on the engagement and the instructor's preferences. A typical frequency for face-to-face interactions is at least once every two weeks, with email or phone conversations occurring more often.

In contrast, IS area interactions generally occur twice: in the beginning when the team is created and in the end to determine student grades. Other IS interactions are likely to occur only if the student has a problem with the team or another student on the team. The SIT area is for interactions that occur when there is a major disagreement between the team and one or more of its members, but is rarely used. If it is needed, it is because there are such serious disagreements in the team that a student has either quit or been removed, and the instructor needs to call all parties together to work out a solution. The last interaction area of our model is ST. Here, issues of team dynamics come into play. Students will be developing a team structure that will include a team leader, team norms, etc., and this area is a forum for these discussions. It is important to remember that PBL emphasizes that each student must be responsible for their own learning. How this happens in student team consulting is through the team structure. Students work in teams so that collective insight will offset individual limitations.[xiv]

Purpose of Fieldwork

Student team consulting offers students an opportunity to integrate their academic and work experiences in the creation of a consulting solution for a client's real world problem. The consulting course provides students with experiential learning in small group dynamics, problem definition, research methodology and application, project management, and in making presentations. In many respects, the course is a sandbox, where students get to be creative and playful, but in a disciplined manner as described above in the consulting model discussion.

Since the purpose of any consulting engagement is to improve the client's condition, clients are encouraged to actively participate in the student consulting process (see the model) and thereby gain useful recommendations. Further, unlike professional consultants, students are usually less experienced and expected to be learning the consulting process as they work on the assignment.

Another important difference between student and non-student consulting is the need for students and clients to follow the calendar of the academic institution. This is not onerous. Rather, it means that there are identifiable beginning and ending points (along with holidays and other breaks) that are defined by the academic calendar. Good planning at the start can accommodate this.

Ethical Considerations

In addition to adhering to the code of ethics of their academic institution, students, clients and instructors need to conduct themselves in such a way that business ethics are strictly observed. If the consulting engagement's methodology calls for primary research, students must clearly identify themselves as students in a student team consulting course of their university, conducting research for the benefit of their identified client. Students should also attest that they have no conflicts of interest with the client's business. Such conflicts can include family members (including self) owning a business that competes with the client, recommending services to the client that the students have a financial interest in, and directly starting a venture that competes with the client. In addition, student should confirm that they have no rights to any improvements in the client's business that may result from the consulting engagement. It is central to the integrity of the student team consulting process that this kind of full disclosure never be compromised.

Confidentiality

Another hallmark of student team consulting is the maintenance of confidentiality. Its purpose is to commit the students and the instructor to treating all materials received and developed during the consulting engagement as the confidential property of the client.

Occasionally a client may have a situation involving intellectual property that counsel advises be covered by a non-standard agreement drawn by the attorney and client. In such instances, the instructor will obtain the institution's advice on using the non-standard form, and students should be free to consult their own attorneys. While the client's rights may justify special treatment, neither the institution nor the students can be unfairly restricted in their future endeavors. Most institutions use a standard form that discusses ethical considerations and confidentiality, similar to the examples in Appendix 2A.

As students begin their consulting assignment, there should be a chronological flow to their approach. Students now can use a process flow model to understand the experiential student team consulting (STC) process. Figure 2 illustrates the complete model, and each main segment will be detailed in a separate chapter.

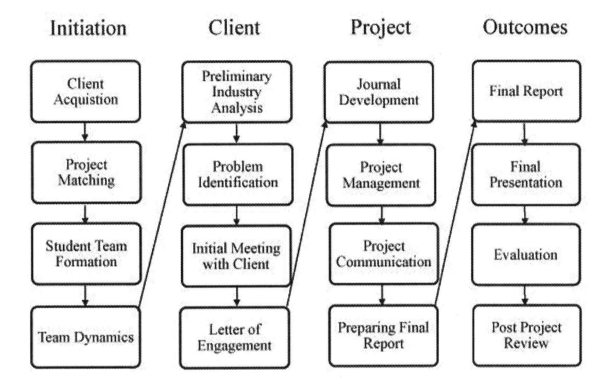

Figure 2 – Process Flow Model

Chapter Three – Process Flow: Initiation

Figure 2a- Process Flow Model

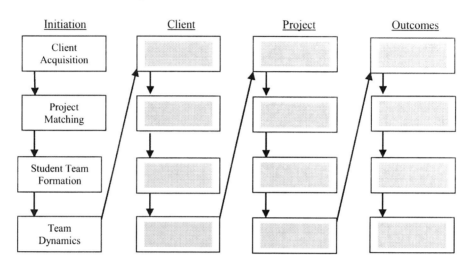

This chapter discusses student teams from client acquisition through team organization, and matches the initiation stage within the Process Flow Model, as depicted in Figure 2a. The team approach is critical to student consulting. Although each student has ideas about how to approach a client's problem, the team context requires students to learn from each another as well as to negotiate to reach a solution. "By collaborating, each team capitalizes on its members' individual strengths and expertise. Teams also learn to handle inevitable disagreements and conflicts."[xv]

Acquisition

Initiation starts with client acquisition. It occurs before the course begins and is usually done by the instructor. It consists of finding a client and ensuring that the client is a good fit for a consulting project. Prospective clients can be generated from a variety of sources such as referrals from previous clients, past students, word of mouth, publicity, and the school's development office.

Once prospects are identified, the instructor needs to screen them to ensure:
- Availability of key personnel to meet with students during the project.
- Willingness to share all relevant information with a student team.
- Understanding the constraints of the academic calendar in both scheduling and conducting an engagement.

The final step in acquisition is creating and signing a contract between the client and the school. This contract typically will detail the milestones, the students' role as consultants, participation fees (if any), possible publicity, and any other items that may be required by the school. It is important to remember that this contract is not about the issues that the students will address in developing the Letter of Engagement as discussed in chapter four.

Matching

Project matching can occur simultaneously with team formation. However, the process here is explained sequentially. Hence, once students are in a student team, they will find themselves in one of three situations:

1) The instructor has assigned a client company to you.
2) Client companies have been selected by the instructor but students have some role in determining which company they want to work with.
3) Students choose from a portfolio of client projects.

In the majority of circumstances, the client has agreed to participate in the consulting program and the student only has the opportunity to influence which project s/he may work on. There are also situations where instructors simply have to assign students to both teams and clients. In other cases, students are able to exercise choice from a menu of client projects, sometimes after the clients have come to the school and make a presentation to the student consultants about their organization and their needs. In cases where this occurs, instructors check for team balance and skills at that time, adjusting as necessary with or without negotiation with the students. Sometimes there's an additional element where a group of students have a pre-existing study group and wish to keep that group intact for the consulting course. When possible, these wishes can be respected, as long as the skills balance and a match with clients can be achieved.

Formation

Student consulting teams can have from two to eight or more members. There is really no set number. This activity often happens simultaneously with project matching. The team size depends in part on the magnitude of the consulting project. Undergraduate, one-semester courses usually have teams of three or four students. Longer programs (sometimes two semesters in length) normally have teams of four to seven students and are more commonly found in graduate programs. To aid in the creation of teams, it is suggested that instructors use some kind of background or profile questionnaire (see Appendix 2B for a template) that is completed by students after registration but before the first class. Instructors use this information to attempt to balance team skills, academic disciplines, career interests, and experience while evaluating the client project assignments. Although it's somewhat of an inexact science, team formation needs to balance a mix of student skills, a client fit and, to the extent possible, student choice.

Team Dynamics

This area consists of a number of team issues, ranging from organization to communication to conflict. To begin, once formed, the student teams need to organize themselves. Specifically, they need to select a team leader, administrator and possibly a treasurer. The team leader will serve as the point person for communications with the client and with the instructor, and the team will determine how communication with the client (formal and informal) will be handled. Let us reemphasize this point: each team should have one member (leader) be the main contact person for the client. The client should know who to contact if a question arises. The client should also have a secondary contact person from the team. This person is used only if the first contact person is unavailable. A typical contact form that can be filled out and left with the client is shown in Appendix 2C.

The team leader will also assume the role of team coordinator, assuring the flow of the team's work. If the team consists of five or more students, the leader will most likely assume an expanded coordination role and take on less of the project workload, per se. The administrator will be responsible for taking and disseminating minutes of all team meetings, and collecting and summarizing weekly activity reports. It's possible that one person can serve as leader and administrator, but experience suggests that the team leader not have other, simultaneous team roles. The treasurer is responsible for monetary issues, if any. If there is a budget, the treasurer will collect receipts and process the team's expense reimbursement from the client. It is okay to combine the administrator and treasurer functions, or not have a treasurer if there are no monetary issues. There may be other formal group roles, depending on team size.

An additional task once teams are formed is for the team to decide the medium, nature and frequency of communications among its members. In addition to the standard email, phone and fax media, web-based instructional tools (such as Blackboard®) serve a useful role in facilitating a learning environment. They generally offer common information exchange areas, secure group sections, and the ability for interactive chat rooms. Basically, students are encouraged to adopt whatever methods that will allow them to achieve effective communications.

Conflict is perhaps an inevitable part of a student team's experience, but it doesn't have to be just a source of tension and distraction.[xvi] It can lead to a way of resolving differences and responding to issues that are causing friction between group members. Conflict can direct the group in ways that members would not have anticipated earlier. Conflict can also be something that tears a group apart and that increases tension among members. However, "if people express their feelings and needs in a positive and constructive way, it reduces anxiety and prevents escalation of conflict."[xvii]

When the team is trying to resolve conflict, it is important to strive toward a win-win solution, as conflict resolution need not result in 'winners and losers'. There are two basic methods to deal with conflict: compromise and mediation.[xviii]

Compromise emphasizes both sides giving up something they want in order to reach a middle ground. This is a good method to use when both parties are willing to listen to the other's position. Mediation uses a neutral third party to assist the team members in voluntarily reaching an agreement. Mediation assumes that the parties know their positions the best and enables them to come up with their own solution. Mediation focuses on things team members can change. You don't try to change someone's beliefs or values. Rather, you change tasks or plans.[xix]

There are numerous types of problems that may cause conflict among the team. A brief discussion of some of the more common problems and suggestions for what to do about them are as follows:

1) Frustration over size of project - At the start of a project, a team can be overwhelmed by the amount of work necessary to complete it. At this point, members are often thinking of the project as an individual endeavor rather than as a group one. They may not realize that the work will be divided up and much easier to handle than they believe. One of the first things to do to overcome this is to divide the project into sub-tasks. Use a project management chart (see the discussion in Chapter Five and Appendix 3A) and brainstorm all of the sub-tasks that will need to be completed in order to finish the project. Establish individual responsibility and deadlines for each sub-task.[xx]

2) Unbalanced participation from team members - If one or two individuals dominate the group discussion, the team will lose its most valuable commodity --the variety of opinions and ideas expressed by its members. While some people are naturally more talkative or comfortable in group situations than others, everyone on the team should be encouraged to participate and no one should be allowed to control all of the team discussion. To offset this, try teambuilding activities in which success requires participation from all members in order to draw out the quieter members. This may open up lines of communication and put members more at ease talking to and sharing ideas with each other. Further, the group could have someone assume the role of gatekeeper during each meeting. The gatekeeper's job is to make sure everyone is given a chance to speak and that no one person dominates the conversation.[xxi]

3) Frustration over lack of progress - When a project takes a long time to complete, team members often feel as though the end will never come and that they haven't accomplished anything. This frustration can also occur when the team comes across a problem that they are having trouble solving. One way to overcome this is to have team members check off the tasks that have been completed from the project management chart, and then they can see how much they have accomplished. You can also ask each member to list two things they have done for the project so far and two things they still need to do. Someone in the group can then record all of the things the team has accomplished and all

of the things they still need to do, and the team can see how far they have come. If your team is really frustrated, then step away from the project for a few minutes. Do something else for 15 minutes to get your minds off of the project.[xxii]

4) Resistance to being a team - There are many reasons why students may resist being part of a team. They could have had negative group experiences in the past, they might fear rejection of their ideas, or they may not trust that the other members will do their share of the work. People who are resistant to working in a team often agree to any idea that the team has in order to get the project done quicker. Further, when people resist being part of the team, they might work on their own and keep their ideas to themselves. As a result, other team members might think that some students are free riding and become resentful. At a minimum, the group loses a valuable resource.

Teambuilding activities that allow members to get to know each other are good for increasing comfort levels within the team. By setting deadlines and asking everyone to give an update of their section of the project at each meeting, team members are able to keep track of each other. This ensures that everyone is doing their part of the work and helps those members who are afraid they will have to do more than their fair share of the work. If many of the people in your team have had negative group experiences, have everyone list two positive things about working with a team. Discuss how you can incorporate those characteristics into your team. You can also have each member name one thing that went wrong with a previous team and discuss how you can avoid having the same problem arise within your team. Establish norms that ensure each member has the opportunity to speak openly and candidly.[xxiii]

5) Separating fact from opinion - When people feel strongly about something, they often will state their personal opinions as facts. While opinions can be very useful in a team, they must be regarded as subjective and you must recognize that not everyone will agree with an opinion. It is important that your team is objective and critical when dealing with opinions so that you do not proceed on unreliable information. A group norm can be instituted where everyone must back their opinions with facts or sources. To implement this, the group could have someone assume the role of devil's advocate at each meeting. This person should question all statements and giving opposing viewpoints so that other team members are required to make sound arguments and think through their statements.[xxiv]

In summary, conflict in student teams is not a question of if; it is a question of when. Students will have different expectations of the project itself, the level of commitment they expect others to put forth, and the level of effort they plan on expending. Dealing with these issues up front is important for the team. If you can't resolve differences in the beginning when everyone is polite and cordial, then later conflicts may be more difficult to resolve.

A final team dynamics task is determining how the team will document its activity through the course. The students should keep track of their time, and summarize it weekly. If it is a large team with a team leader who serves as a coordinator, the team administrator should collect and summarize these weekly reports, and provide them to the team leader. During the project, these activity logs will help the team leader and the instructor monitor team activity, so as to facilitate action as needed to help distribute workloads more equitably. At the end, regardless of team size, the team leader will provide a summary activity report of total hours spent by the team on the project to the instructor. This is a useful number to document the value of the consulting engagement to the client. The value is a simple calculation of total hours multiplied by the prevailing local hourly consulting rate. See Appendix 2D for a sample activity log.

Chapter Four – Process Flow: Client

Figure 2b- Process Flow Model

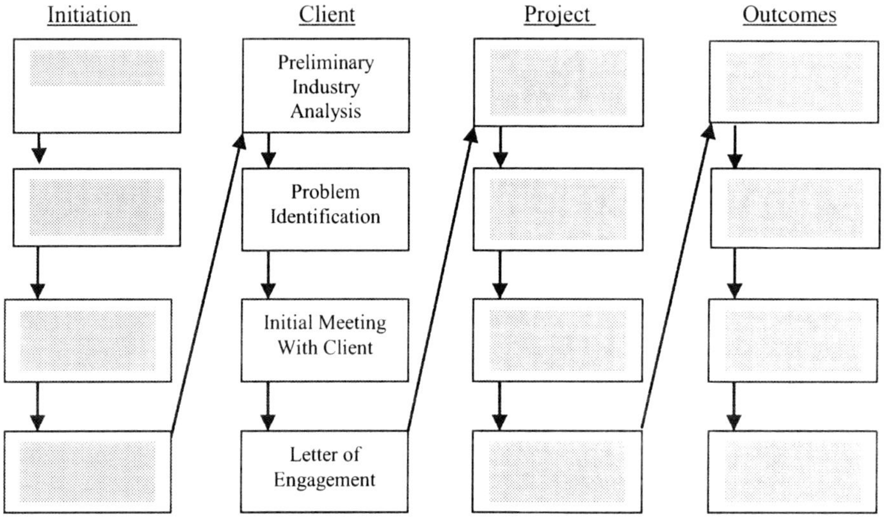

Initiation	Client	Project	Outcomes
	Preliminary Industry Analysis		
	Problem Identification		
	Initial Meeting With Client		
	Letter of Engagement		

In this chapter, the client phase of the Process Flow model (Figure 2b) is discussed as students learn how to manage client relations. As discussed in the previous chapter on initiation, the consulting process also requires an understanding of the needs and interests of the client. This phase entails gathering information about the firm and its industry, understanding client problems and issues, the initial client meeting, and preparing the Letter of Engagement (LOE).

Preliminary Industry Analysis

The traditional business school approach to situation analysis has long been to use SWOT analysis, where SWOT stands for "Strengths, Weaknesses, Opportunities and Threats." The first two, of course, are internal to the firm while the latter two are external. The typical SWOT approach has been to ask questions of the firm in S, W, O and T order.

It is recommended that you reverse the SWOT approach and conduct a TOWS analysis. This asks that you first consider the external elements (threats and opportunities) in order to develop the context within which to examine the internal elements (weaknesses and strengths). TOWS analysis thus rests on the notion that a firm's strengths and weaknesses are only relevant within the context of the firm's environment. To illustrate, consider the Olympic swimmer who's dropped into the middle of the Pacific or the Sahara. That the person is an Olympic-class swimmer would normally be a strength. But within the context of the mid-Pacific or mid-Saharan environment, it doesn't matter.

When beginning the first step of the client phase, industry analysis, students generally know very little about the firm or its industry. Quickly getting up to speed is important. An excellent strategy would be to involve the business librarian at the beginning of the industry analysis. This would mean the team would have access to the best resources available and would have expert research guidance. A team should conduct a TOWS analysis of the firm as the foundation to understanding the environment in which the firm operates. Students should undertake this analysis in the spirit of inquiry, not advocacy. A TOWS analysis is a process of discovery, not judgment.

There are numerous models to help assess the general environment.[xxv] Michael Porter's five forces concept is one of the most useful.[xxvi] Other models can also help the team use a framework to develop a briefing paper. This paper is a working document consisting of an overview of the client's industry (industry trends) and a competition comparison. This briefing paper allows students to place the firm and its issues into a proper, real world context. Without knowledge of the client's environment, students may make recommendations that are simply not relevant. Beginning this research before meeting the client allows the team to begin a background analysis without potential client biases.

For example, industry trends should include recent events in the industry and describe the industry structure and size. Is the industry dominated by large or small firms? Is the overall industry expanding? How is money made in this business? What is the fixed versus variable cost structure? Teams should use the questions in Appendix 1A, and be sure to cite sources to improve the plan's credibility. As an example, see the following excerpt from an industry trends discussion done by the student team who completed the project in Appendix 3B:

Revenue for the industry from 2009 to 2010 is expected to increase by 5.1% to $18.45 billion. Unfortunately this represents only a partial recovery from the fall in demand that was experienced as a result of the economic recession (IBIS World, 2010). As corporate profits were squeezed during the recession, so were the budgets of these corporations and institutions. As a result, businesses began cutting back spending where ever possible.

The largest market for this industry is Janitorial Services. The providers of these services purchase cleaning products in bulk from wholesalers in this industry. In 2009, revenues of companies within the Janitorial Services Industry declined 5.2%. The falling demand for janitorial services directly led to the falling demand of cleaning supplies and equipment required by the purchase from wholesalers. The amount of cleaning supplies and equipment required by the janitorial and custodial service company's was also affected by the increased vacancy rate of offices, shopping centers and factories that occurred in the midst of the recession (IBIS World, 2010).

While industry demand is expected to improve from 2010 to 2011 as the economy continues to recover (by 2.1% to $18.84 billion), businesses in the industry will still have its challenges. It is expected that an increased number of clients will continue to bypass wholesalers and instead purchase equipment and supplies directly from the manufacturer. As more clients purchase products directly from manufacturers, the industry has experienced more and more consolidations. This has forced existing wholesalers to take part in the price competition which reduces their profit margins (IBIS World, 2010). Also while the economic recession had impacted this industry overall, new trends within the industry were beginning to emerge. Despite the impact of the economy, a 2009 report by Green Seal and Enviromedia Social Marketing revealed that 58% of consumers were buying green cleaning products. Also, 19% of the 1,000 people surveyed noted that they are actually buying more green products in 2009 than before the recession (Williamson, 2009).

In the competition comparison, students need to address the key competitors' strengths and weaknesses. At a minimum, this should be four primary competitors. In circumstances where there are not four primary competitors, utilize secondary competitors. For example, if the client was a fitness center, then the competitors would be other fitness centers. If four centers do not exist in the client's market area, then the team could consider individuals who work out at home as competition, or use another type of fitness facility like a rock climbing gym. Next, from the industry trends section, the team would identify key industry success factors and construct a comparison chart that ranks these factors against the client and client's competitors. For example, here is a chart based on a project looking at the market for vehicle oil changes, developed by a student team:

Comparative Advantages of Oil-Lubrication Market Segments					
Segment					
Parameter	DIY	Dealer/OEM	Full/ Limited Service	Fast- Lube	Client
Convenience (time)	Lowest	Mid/High	High	High	Highest
Convenience (location)	N/A	Lowest	High	High	Highest
Cost of Service	Lowest	Highest	Mid	Mid	Mid
Mkt Sector Growth	N/A	Slow/Level	Declining	High/ Leveling	Mid/ Growing
Operating/ Entry Cost	N/A	Highest	High	Low	Lowest
Reputation	N/A	Highest	High	Mid	Mid
Customer Loyalty	N/A	High	Mid	Mixed	Mid
Mfg. Support	N/A	Highest	High	Mixed	Mid

Understanding both the industry and the competition allows the team to better identify issues and problems, and after research, offer better recommendations.

Problem Identification

Typically, the student team, along with the client, needs to identify the root problem(s) facing the firm or organization.[xxvii] This activity is critical to the effectiveness of the consulting project. Business owner/managers sometimes focus on treating the symptoms rather than the root problems. They are so busy managing the business that they may not have time or skills for the kind of analysis that will uncover the underlying problem. Owner/managers' egos may also get in the way of examining the business objectively.

For example, an owner who is in a cash crunch may conclude that the best solution is to get a loan as soon as possible. However, the short-term loan relief could temporarily hide an underlying problem such as deteriorating turnover of accounts receivables. Treating the symptom in this case would only delay the consequences of the problem and probably exacerbate the financial condition of the business by adding a greater debt load to a diminishing cash flow. By contrast, identifying the reasons for slower receivables could lead to recommendations that would boost collections. The resulting increase in cash flow could reduce or eliminate the need for borrowing.

To find the underlying problems, the student team will need to look at the probable causes and analyze each of these areas. Appendix 1A has a sampling of some useful inquiry areas. This appendix can be used as an idea generator for the team. Your client and the environment in which it operates will influence the question areas.

Benchmarks such as industry and historical ratios can also help the team zero in on problem areas. For example, if the gross margin for a business is 20% when the industry norm is 40%, an analysis may turn up problems with pilferage, improper markup procedures, a high level of returns, or other causes. Through research, inquiry, and analysis, the team should narrow down the list of probable causes in order to determine the actual root problems.

Another issue that may arise with the client is a lack of cooperation regarding data access. In a student consulting engagement, it is expected that the client will provide needed information to the team in a timely manner. During a typical semester, there is no extra time to wait for the client to provide data. A delay is costly if a team has to scramble to make up for lost time. What should students do if the client fails to provide needed information to the team?

First, notify the instructor. The instructor and team then determine how to handle the situation. The second step is to proceed with as much of the project as can be done without the data, in the hope that the information will be forthcoming. If the issue persists, the third step is to adjust the project parameters so client data are not necessary to complete the project. This needs to be done only with the permission and assistance of the instructor, and in consultation with the client.

Unfortunately, clients are sometimes unresponsive in field case consulting projects. The clients' lack of responsiveness early on, if allowed to continue, can be an indicator of how the project will go. The solution in these circumstances may be to replace the unresponsive client with another one. Fortunately, these glitches are relatively rare since most clients are very responsive to the team's needs. After all, the team's goal is to help the client's business.

Another issue that may arise between the client and the team is different expectations as to the scope of the project due to the ambiguous nature of a consulting assignment. Scope creep occurs where the client believes the team will be working on a certain set of activities and that those activities keep expanding due to the fluid nature of a consulting assignment. Meanwhile, the team is operating on a different set of assumptions. If this occurs, teams need to immediately communicate with the instructor and the client as the project evolves. The key is clarity in the nature of what is to be done and that occurs in a clearly delineated letter of engagement (LOE), which is the contract negotiated between the team and the client at the beginning of the engagement. The LOE is discussed further in this chapter. It helps prevent confusion about what is to be done, and should describe how any changes in the scope of work will be handled.

Initial Client Meeting

Once the student consulting team has gathered information from secondary sources, created a briefing paper, and developed questions, it's time to meet the client. It is a good practice to meet with the client only after you have a reasonable understanding of the general environment in which the firm operates.

Students should dress professionally and begin this first meeting by giving the client a signed confidentiality agreement and completed group contact sheet (see Appendices 2A & 2C). There are two possibilities for the first meeting. If the engagement begins with the client(s) meeting the student team(s) in the classroom, then the instructor will be present and generally will observe the teams. The second meeting will then occur at the client's business with just the students present. If the first meeting occurs at the client's business, the instructor should not attend this client meeting. The student team is the professional consultant in this arrangement, and if the instructor accompanies the students, the focus changes from the student team to the instructor.

As the industry research should have been completed or substantially underway at this point, students can use some of this information to help the discussion by asking more informed questions. This should allow you to get to the primary purpose of this meeting, namely, to understand the clients' needs in order to negotiate the problem definition for the project. This will be the foundation for the LOE. After a tour of the facilities, students use this opportunity to address key questions: How does the client envision this consulting assignment? What types of issues need to be addressed? What outcome does the client want? The following elements are from the project example in Appendix 3B:

- Make strategic business recommendations to effectively tap into the consumer market for Spruce's private label and eco-friendly cleaning products.
- Conduct research with consumers and retailers to provide input on what consumers' demand of an eco-friendly cleaning product.
- Create a marketable brand of eco-friendly cleaning products that will appeal to the consumer market.
- Provide suggestion on how to utilize the Strictly Quarts consumer website.

Letter of Engagement (LOE)

Clients may or may not have a good grasp of their needs. They may be focusing on the symptoms of a problem but not the root cause. Thus, it is important to probe deeply in order to develop a clear understanding of their situation. The LOE negotiations can then be started. The LOE must include:

1) The project objective(s) – what does the team intend to do?
2) The approach – how does the team intend to do it? With what milestones and at what cost?
3) The deliverables – what will the client receive from the project?

The problem definition comes from a clear understanding of the client's needs. The LOE identifies what you are going to do, why, and by when. It provides all parties with a clear statement of the outcomes of the problem-based learning (PBL) activity.[xxviii] What needs to be researched? What issues have to be resolved? For example, see the excerpt for Spruce Industries:

Project Objective(s)

Spruce currently sells and distributes cleaning products to businesses or organizations that use the products purchased for industrial purposes. With intense competition in this market, including product price cutting due to the recession, it is becoming increasingly difficult for Spruce to discover new business opportunities. Spruce would like KJP Consulting to make strategic business recommendations to effectively tap into the consumer market, specifically for their in-house (private label) and eco-friendly cleaning supplies.

To accomplish that objective, Spruce is looking to expand the consumer market through retail outlets. While this has never been attempted by Spruce, KJP Consulting will research if there is a significant opportunity to grow the revenue of the firm by obtaining shelf-space in retail outlets.

In order to develop a plan that will reach this market, the Student Consulting Team will conduct research with consumers and retailers to create a marketable brand of eco-friendly cleaning products that will appeal to the consumer market. This will entail creating a new brand name, and designing new packaging.

In contrast, the approach is a methodology question. How does the team intend to meet the objectives? The team needs to be specific as to how they will accomplish the objectives. What is the approach? Since all projects normally have a secondary research component, what will that entail? What sources will be used? Will the team be conducting primary research? If so, what type (interview, survey, observation), and what are the details of that research process? For example, see the excerpt from Spruce Industries:

Approach

In order to meet the objectives of this project, KJP will conduct primary research that looks at retailers of eco-friendly products and how the products they carry are marketed and priced. Part of this analysis will focus on process and its potential to create an advantage. For example, one competitive advantage that Spruce's private label eco-friendly brand products could have over some other consumer-based products is the necessary "green" certifications. Once this research is completed, a brand needs to be created that is appealing to the consumer in terms of product use, brand name, and packaging. Misco Product Corporation will be the source that will provide valuable information on private label branding and packaging to KJP Consulting. Five possible brand names that the consulting team has created will be surveyed in the consumer market using the services of Survey Monkey, to get a sample size of approximately 100 consumers. Based on the popularity of the brand names, they will be narrowed down and then the consulting team will make the final decision as to which name to utilize.

While Spruce's eco-friendly consumer brand is being developed, primary research will be performed concurrently to determine the processes involved and feasibility in obtaining shelf space at various regional and/or local retailers. This primary research will consist of directly contacting two big box retailers (Target and Wal-Mart), two supermarkets (Wegmans and Whole Foods) and two environmentally conscious retail stores (located in New Hope, Pennsylvania area) through phone, email and onsite visits to obtain as much information as possible the feasibility of obtaining shelf-space at these locations

---

The third element in the LOE, deliverables, tells the client what will be received from the team. The instructor and the client are expecting the team to produce the deliverables in the LOE. Thus, a note of caution. Student consulting contracts often tend to promise more than can be delivered, or tend to be less specific. Therefore, different expectations as to what is a quality deliverable might result from a vaguely worded LOE. A high quality engagement that is narrowly defined is better than a poor quality project that addresses too many areas. Quality, not quantity, is crucial. The deliverables will be provided to the client in two ways - in a final written report and a presentation. Appendix 3A provides LOE examples.

There are usually three levels that the student team has to be concerned with when developing the LOE. Larger firms tend to have more complex organizational structures and more people who may be affected by implementation of the team's recommendations. Students should thus consider the following issues:

> 1) How to deal with the client's definition of the problem? The client may be describing symptoms instead of the root cause(s). How does the student team handle the situation if they disagree with the client's assessment?

> 2) How to deal with the underlying organizational issues that may have caused the problem? These are situations where the firm's structure is faulty.

> 3) How to handle any politics of the situation? Who might be affected by your proposed changes? Is the situation workable?

A last issue to consider in the LOE is reimbursement to the students for out of pocket expenses. Costs that are expected to occur during a project are the client's responsibility. Your instructor may ask you to prepare a pro-forma budget proposal for client approval and to include a summary of that budget in the LOE. Typical expenses include travel, parking, telephone, and duplication/binding cost. To the extent that much of the research may be secondary, there may be little or no cost. In some cases, the client has paid a participation fee and normal expenses may be covered under that fee. However, since potential expenses are often unknown at the beginning of a consulting engagement, typical language in a budget request could simply suggest a spending limit and require client approval before any monies are expended above that limit, or for any special purchases related to the consulting engagement. If there is a budget, then the team's treasurer is responsible for it.

Chapter Five – Process Flow: Project

Figure 2c- Process Flow Model

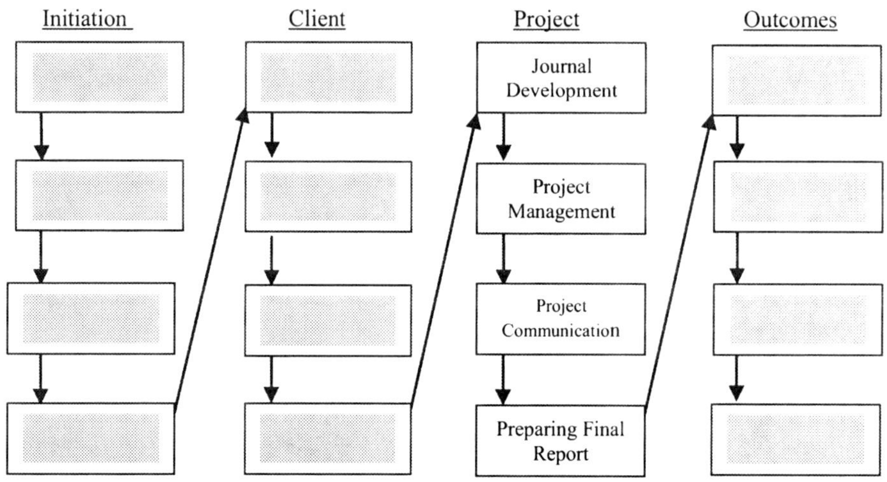

Initiation	Client	Project	Outcomes
		Journal Development	
		Project Management	
		Project Communication	
		Preparing Final Report	

This chapter will cover the project phase, beginning with journal development, project management, communication mechanisms, and preparing the final report.

Journal Development

The individual student journal is an important part of the course and is initiated at the beginning of the project. This journal provides the basis for individual student assessment based on the course learning goals, and is discussed more completely in chapter eight. Sections of the journal need to demonstrate the student's level of understanding of the project at various, pre-determined stages, from measuring the student's baseline knowledge of consulting through reflection about the client's relationship to the community. Additional questionnaires are used to assess the student's progress on the learning goals. The reflection in these journals is one measure of a student's critical thinking and is useful for all types of clients.

Project Management

Once the LOE has been finalized by the client, student team, and instructor, it is time to implement the plan. The team should have developed a general map of the project in the LOE, one that uses a project management process (see LOE in Appendix 3A). This allows tasks to be broken down into specific action steps, with beginning and ending dates for each step, and the student(s) responsible for that step. If primary research is the methodology and the team is surveying a student population at a college for dining preferences (i.e., if the client was a food service provider), some specific action steps might include:

- Identify the student body parameters (on-campus only, full-time or part-time, etc.)
- Develop a mechanism to reach the sample population (campus mail, intercept interview techniques, etc.)
- Design a survey instrument (with assistance from instructor)
- Conduct a pilot test of survey on student sample (if time permits)
- Revise and edit the survey
- Administer the survey
- Conduct data entry of survey returns
- Analyze the data
- Develop findings from the data

If primary research is not the best methodology for the project, then a secondary research protocol typically includes internet exploration, database searches, company research, etc., preferably under the guidance of the business librarian as discussed earlier in the industry analysis. The point here is to break down the project into discrete steps with a student(s) responsible for each part, and a start/completion date.

Most of the above student population survey research has additional steps. For example, survey design has a number of actions such as topic selection, survey length, specific question structure, etc. Further, the larger the number of students on the team, the more important it is to breakout the project into this level of detail as coordination among larger teams is very critical.

Finally, the team needs to avoid operating as a "one week wonder," i.e., delaying work on the project until near the end of the semester and then pulling all-nighters, etc., to finish. The use of a project management approach helps keep the team on track.

Project Communication

As the project takes shape, there are a number of key issues that will emerge. Among the first is instructor/team communication. Progress reports should be made by the team leader or designated team member to the instructor on a weekly or bi-weekly basis. These can be submitted electronically (see Appendix 2E). In this report, there can be sections to describe the team's output and each individual student's activities. This allows the instructor to monitor individual's contributions to the team effort. For example, see the following sample progress report:

TEAM/STUDENT PROGRESS REPORT (submit 1 per team)

Team name: XXXXXX_____   Date:2/22/12_____

INTERVIEWS:

Name of firm_____   Person interviewed_____

Type of interview: at firm____   telephone____   other _____

Group members present/involved: _____
1) Purpose of interview (goals):
2) Information obtained:

TEAM ACTIVITY (not the interview):
1) Describe any work done this week(s) related to the project:
The letter of engagement, project outline, and signature page were completed.

2) Indicate the sources used in any research that was done:
We used blackboard and the textbook for templates of Letters of Engagement.

3) Describe any problem areas you have encountered associated with the project. Have they been successfully overcome?

INDIVIDUAL ACTIVITY (each team member should list his/her name and what they did during this reporting period involving their consulting project):

1) Student 1

I completed the "how does the team intend to do it" section and I looked up an example of the outline of the project so it can be completed on time.

2) Student 2

I wrote the background, project objectives, and project budget sections of the letter of engagement. I also put together the LOE and the signature page.

3) Student 3

I wrote the "what we are going to give the client" this included the client deliverables as well as what our business is plan is going to include once we present our report to client. I also wrote out the project guidelines showing what responsibilities both the student consulting team and the client will have throughout the project.

Teams may have a standard meeting time with the instructor. At these meetings, the student team needs to be prepared to discuss project execution, possible scheduling glitches, and any other problems. Problems should be caught early. Proper project management can provide the structure needed to let the students know if they are on track. Another important tool is the weekly activity report, a summary of the week's hours spent by the students. This activity log helps the instructor monitor student activity and take corrective action, especially if it appears that students are spending too much time. Students can and do get carried away with projects. These time summaries should be expressed in incremental hours for the week as well as cumulative hours for the engagement. As mentioned earlier, at the end of the project, the team can multiply its total project hours by the prevailing local hourly consulting rate to give the client an indication of the comparable value received from the student consulting team.

Clients, too, need progress reports. The nature and frequency of these reports is defined in the LOE, as fieldwork assignments can vary greatly in scope and duration. The team and the client are encouraged to develop their own reporting arrangements, while recognizing that progress report writing is adjunct to the consulting process, and is not the process itself. In addition to whatever progress reports the team and client choose to adopt, there are generally two formal client reports. The first of these is the LOE. This can be signed and mailed, or presented to the client face-to-face. The second formal report is the final presentation itself. Additional comments on the final report will be found later in the chapter.

Another option for a possible third formal report is an interim presentation to the client to report progress to date, and the anticipated next steps. As noted, the client will want to be kept informed of the project's progress, and an interim report can do this. However, an interim report may not be appropriate in situations where plan execution takes most of semester and there truly are no interim results. The student team may still be exploring different avenues and any findings could be misleading to the client. Therefore, for term or shorter length assignments, a formal interim report might not be viable.

Preparing Final Report

Based on the LOE and its project management timeline, the project may be broken down into draft sections of the final report. The students and the instructor should find it mutually beneficial to utilize evaluative feedback loops, based on the students submitting to the instructor sections of the project as homework. Students then have an opportunity to operationalize the final report with the knowledge that a large portion of their project has received written feedback by the instructor. Homework assignments can be the LOE and the two sections of the report, plus any other sections deemed appropriate by the instructor.

At the conclusion of the engagement, the team will prepare its final written report and presentation to the client (see chapter six). Once a set of tentative conclusions and recommendations has been drafted, it's time to ask the "so what" question. The team needs to rigorously question its findings for relevance - what's important, why is it important, how will implementing this report's findings improve the situation of the client? Why does it matter? There must be a clear enough answer to the "so what" question for the final report and presentation to be meaningful to the client and the team.

Chapter Six – Project Flow: Outcomes

Figure 2d - Process Flow Model

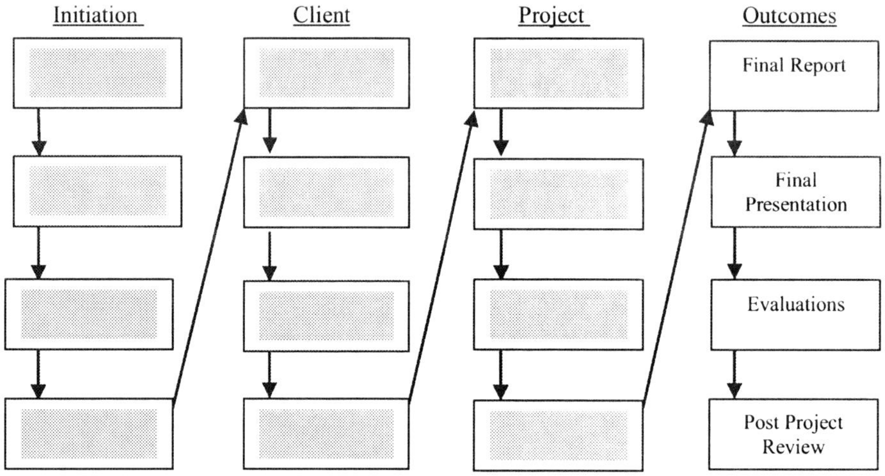

This chapter will discuss wrapping up the student team consulting project. It includes the final written report, the final presentation, evaluations and post project review.

Final Report

The flow of the report should build upon the sections turned in earlier for feedback, which are now finalized. Each report's content and structure will depend on the nature of the consulting engagement as depicted in the LOE. However, the preferred flow of the final report is an executive summary, problem definition, company description, industry overview, review of research methodology, summary of research results, conclusions and recommendations, and appendices. See Appendix 3B for sample final reports.

One of the most frequently asked questions about the final report is its length. On one hand, the answer is as long as necessary to state and defend your conclusions and recommendations. On the other hand, most reports will fall into the 40 to 60 pages range, plus appendices. The report should be professional in appearance and appropriate to the client. Longer reports may be likely if the assignment is a comprehensive overview of an organization vs. a focused effort on one or two areas. The team should give the instructor its final report for review/grading prior to presenting it to the client. After this review, and at the final presentation, the instructor and each representative of the client should receive a final bound copy. An important and collegial closure to the project can often be accomplished with a simple, but formal thank you note from the team to the client. The note can be most effective if it is given as the absolute last activity of the final presentation meeting and it is given separately from the final written report. Although most teams know what they want to say, an example can be found in the Appendix 3D.

<u>Final Presentation</u>

The final presentation is essentially the explanation of the written report's executive summary. It should be crafted to follow the old sales process of tell them what you're going to tell them, tell them, and tell them what you've told them. Delivering the final presentation is a very important part of the learning process for the students. As such, all students should participate. One effective way to present is for the team leader to introduce the presentation and team, tell the client what they are going to hear, and then come back to wrap it up (tell them what they heard) after the other students have presented their sections. The team should decide whether it wishes to allow the client to ask questions during the presentation or hold them until the end. Holding until the end typically allows for a better flow as all students will usually be presenting.

The length can vary based on the complexity of the project and the number of students on the team but a typical presentation time is about an hour, including time for questions and answers. Students should be dressed professionally. A photo shoot with the client and the students is also a great publicity opportunity. Pictures can be posted on the web or on social media, and sent to other media outlets. The university can gain excellent publicity from these outreach efforts.

In addition, the student team should, by themselves, do a dry run of their presentation to check on timing, flow, and, content. It also affords the chance to see if the "so what" question has been asked and answered. Most teams will find it useful to also have a dry run with the instructor, perhaps videotaped for later critique. Presentations to the client always benefit from practicing at least once as a group. A PowerPoint presentation for one of the sample consulting reports is in Appendix 3C. A partial sample from that presentation is as follows:

Spruce Industries, Inc.

Clean With The Power Of Green

A Feasibility Study on Entering the Consumer Market for "Green" Cleaning Products

Presented by:

the Rider University Student Consulting Team

Project Description

The objective of this consulting project is to provide Spruce with strategic business recommendations as it relates to penetrating the consumer market for "green" cleaning products, as follows:

• Private-label Branding

• Product Line

• Process & Feasibility of Obtaining Retail Shelf-Space

• Consumer Website

• Final Recommendations

Evaluations

In the student consulting process, one of the last activities is the evaluation. This step in the process model can consist of up to four evaluations whose purpose is to provide feedback to the students and instructor. Feedback is important to the students because this may be their first fieldwork experience. As a result, they may develop insights that will help them to improve their interpersonal skills and abilities. Feedback is important to the instructor because it helps in a continuous improvement process. The instructor can assess the responses as to what worked and what did not as an aid to improving the consulting experience in the future. Evaluations also provide data to the instructor to help calculate the student's grade, although weights for various types of evaluations can vary substantially. There are four basic types of evaluations discussed here: peer, client's team, instructor's individual, and instructor's team. Not every consulting program will use all evaluations.

Peer Evaluation - The most common formal evaluation is the peer assessment (see Appendix 2F). At times during the course, and always at the conclusion of the consulting project, students will evaluate their team members and themselves. The key to this evaluation is to focus on the behavior of the team member during the project and not on his/her personality. Some members of the team may not get along with other members, and tend to rate those individuals unfavorably. Focusing on behaviors can help separate performance from personality and overcome that bias.

These evaluations should be confidential and anonymous, and used by the instructor to compute part of the student's grade. Since most of the consulting assignment is team based, most grading points will be based on team output. The peer evaluation helps the instructor measure the individual's performance in a group setting. Further, as students often are concerned with any "free riders" in a group, a peer evaluation can help an individual student's grade better reflect that student's efforts and results. Peer evaluations can also be useful for self-improvement if there is a consensus among the team that a student has a deficiency in an area. This can be particularly helpful for a mid-term course correction. The instructor can then share the team's concerns in the aggregate with the affected student, and not identify specific comments from the peer evaluations. Key point: the confidential nature of this evaluation must be protected if honest responses are desired. In addition, even if a peer evaluation is done only at the end of the term, the feedback can still help the student in future endeavors.

Client's Team Evaluation - This formal report allows the client to evaluate the project based upon performance of the consulting team. It usually involves completing a rating form, which assesses the final report, the presentation, and the overall performance of the consulting team (see Appendix 2F). The comments are generally used to help the instructor understand the team's performance from the client's perspective. The team rating can be used by the instructor for computing individual team members' grades. Although a client may get to know some members of the team well enough to provide specific comments about individuals, generally this feedback applies only to the entire team. This is also a very common evaluation. How this feedback is used in an instructor's grading procedures will vary based on the instructor. As noted earlier, the instructor can also use client observations to improve the consulting experience for future engagements.

Instructor's Team Evaluation- In this evaluation, the team is assessed on its performance directly by the instructor.   This evaluation is an ongoing process that occurs through homework assignments (if used) and outcomes of team/instructor meetings, as well as by grades on the presentation and final written report. In addition, unlike the client evaluation, this feedback can be timely so that the team can make corrections during the course of the consulting engagement.

In evaluating team performance, there are generally two elements. First, the team is judged on the outputs that it produces, i.e., did the team produce the deliverables as promised in the LOE? This is often based on any homework assignments, the final written report and presentation. Second, consideration is given to the team dynamics, the team's process for handling issues, and the team's ability to improve its process during the engagement period. Since this part of the assessment is subjective, team members need to focus on communicating effectively with the instructor, the client, and each other.

Instructor's Individual Evaluation- This evaluation is used both formally and informally. It is formal when a specific mechanism (usually a rubric) is used by the instructor to evaluate an individual's performance. This evaluation of the individual's contribution is usually based on team meetings, the presentation, progress reports, etc. Often this appraisal, along with peer evaluation, becomes the individual assessment in the grading system. When the evaluation is used for feedback, the instructor shares these ratings with the student. Timing is also important so that early feedback allows students to make corrections during the course. End of project feedback shifts this emphasis to helping the student be better prepared for future experiences.

Informally, the instructor's individual evaluation will always be part of the course grading. For purposes of this book, however, the focus is on formal evaluations. They provide a basis for discussion in feedback situations and a set of criteria for establishing fair assessment of student performance. For examples of client and peer evaluations, see Appendix 2F.

Post Project Review

At this time, the team should be wrapping up its experiential consulting project. Our "sandbox" approach allows students tremendous flexibility to develop unique solutions, yet it follows a logical, pedagogically sound framework for the integrative demands of experiential learning.

One of the most interesting aspects of this learning experience is the "rest of the story." Unlike hypothetical cases or business plans, a team's consulting report is for a real organization. The process depicted is designed to assist students, clients and instructors. By its nature, it does not include any student activity after the course ends.   So, the question remains: Does the organization implement the student team recommendations?

As might be surmised, this is one of the most common queries posed by students. Therefore, we encourage students to work with their instructors to develop a follow-up mechanism that allows students to learn the results of their hard work on behalf of the client. For example, one of the authors utilizes a client impact survey that is given to his clients one to one and a half years after they have finished their STC experience to learn if recommendations have been implemented, and what were the results. This survey is administered at the end of the academic year for projects that were done in the previous academic year. An example of this survey is in Appendix 2G.

This is just one possibility of tracking client results. Depending on the school and STC program, a school may want to follow up annually (or a different time frame) with the same clients for a number of years, simply conduct a one-time survey, or do some other measure. Whatever mechanism is used, it is important to track STC effectiveness from the client perspective. This type of information can be invaluable in promoting the program, recruiting new clients, and demonstrating the importance of this activity internally at your school.

Chapter Seven: Service-learning and the Student Team Consulting Model

What is Service-Learning

Service-learning is a method of teaching, learning and reflecting in the community.[xxix] In their book, Where's the Learning in Service-learning?, Eyler and Giles talk about some common characteristics shared by service-learning experiences:

- They address complex problems in complex settings rather than simplified problems in isolation.
- They offer opportunities to practice critical thinking.
- They involve collaborative experiences and promote skills related to teamwork and community involvement.
- They promote deeper learning because the results are immediate and real.[xxx]

Service-learning helps students develop critical reflection, increases their understanding of social problems, and enhances their teamwork abilities.[xxxi] Engagement in service-learning has been shown to increase students' commitment to service, and improve their communication skills and social issue awareness. [xxxii] As demonstrated by the Community Food Bank example (Appendix 3B), the STC model is a perfect framework for service-learning in a business school environment.

The experiential student team consulting approach discussed here shares a number of important characteristics with service-learning. Both are focused on problem-based learning in a cooperative (team) environment. Both focus on building critical thinking skills and typically offer an inter-disciplined approach to complex issues. More specifically, service-learning in the management area is also a process-based approach that focuses on students taking on "the role of professional consultants producing goods that will, in fact, be used (p.59)."[xxxiii] Given the shared characteristics, we find strong synergy between experiential student team consulting and service-learning.

Lessons From Student Team Consulting for Service-Learning

On their own, and also responding to the requirements of the AACSB, business schools have been including courses in ethics and social responsibility in their curriculum.[xxxiv] The STC model can provide opportunities for learning in these areas by creating turnkey projects in the service-learning field. In general, our methodology can help faculty handle service-learning projects, provide integration into a course, create value for all stakeholders, is grounded in real world projects, and greatly enhances the students' cognitive abilities. One service-learning approach, advocated by Dumas (p.254), is the four-step "preparation, service, reflection, and celebration" method of designing service-learning projects[xxxv]. The STC model can facilitate effective learning-based connections between student experience, course content, and community.

For example, in a study of service-learning partnership preferences, almost two-thirds of community organization members' were interested in transactional, or one time projects with university partnership programs, typically because of resource constraints (e.g., staff time). These transactional projects typically do not require much investment on the part of either party.[xxxvi] The fieldwork approach in our book is designed with these transactional aspects in mind, making it ideally suited to working in this kind of a service-learning environment. The STC approach provides starting and stopping points designed around an academic calendar, and requires the students, faculty and client to have an agreed understanding of the tasks the students are to accomplish. The student team consulting model requires a Letter of Engagement (LOE) that spells out the respective responsibilities, and provides clarity to the engagement. As the service-learning environment has had difficulty documenting the learning process,[xxxvii] the LOE is one tool that can help demonstrate how learning will occur. The student journal also serves as an assurance of learning tool (see Chapter 8) but it also can be a vehicle for deeper reflection of service-learning topics such as ethical business practices, or the impact of volunteerism, to name but a few options choices.

The LOE can also be used to communicate with both the administration of the business school and the administration of the college or university. Since it provides the clarity of the relationship between an organization and the STC, this relationship can easily be explained to other parties. Should the administration wish to engage in long-term, university-community partnerships, the STC projects can easily be extended into longer, broader efforts. It is not uncommon for organizations to have iterative STC projects, and based on the projects' recommendations, other departments of the business school such as marketing or advertising may wish to be become engaged with the organization as well. In addition, the use of STC documents can be the easily understood framework for projects that go beyond the business school. For example, a student team could make recommendations to changes in the outreach efforts of a literacy program, and those changes could be effected by a student team from the graphic arts department. The keys to success in service-learning are communication among all the stakeholders and an agreement of the parameters of the project. Both are integral to the STC model.

Lessons from Service-learning to Experiential Student Team Consulting

The emphasis on reflection is a major part of the service-learning model. It is the primary vehicle that demonstrates assurance of learning, and it ensures that the student is not merely another pair of volunteer hands but is applying the service-learning experience to generate a greater understanding. If the STC project is not a service-learning opportunity but instead, is with a for-profit organization, this does not mean that the deeper reflection is of no value. Student team consulting can use reflection as the tool through which students take their application of skills, and translate it into knowledge.[xxxviii] Any organization, either for profit or not-for-profit, faces many choices that have societal effects. Students responsible for any project will benefit from using reflection to look beyond the corporation or organization to its place in the wider world.

Chapter Eight - Assurance of Learning for Experiential Courses

This chapter explains an assurance of learning model for experiential learning courses. This model is important as students typically receive less individual assessments of their skills in problem-based learning (PBL) courses because the majority of the deliverables are team products.[xxxix] The model's purpose is to assist and assess individual student learning during the completion of team-based experiential learning courses.

Our inclusion of this model stems from AACSB standards. AACSB has stated that schools must demonstrate that learning occurs for each learning goal that the school has established.[xl] This necessitates the establishment of defined learning goals and methods to measure the quality of individual student learning which has occurred. This creates a challenge for those facilitating team-based experiential learning courses, like the ones this text is designed to help. While classes such as student consulting programs seem to exemplify the goals of experiential learning, the need to determine strategies to measure what learning has occurred in these programs can be an issue.

Assurance of Learning Model

This model provides assurance of learning during and after an experiential learning course. Items one and two provide the broad parameters of this approach, and are followed by a detailed breakdown of the components. This includes learning goals and a rubric to assess comprehension.

Summary of Requirements

1. **Journal:** This journal is prepared independently by each student. It includes responses to pre-designed surveys given at select times throughout the experiential learning project as well as self-reflective entries. To help ensure that students put forth the needed effort to produce useful data for analysis, students should be informed that part of their final grade will be based upon the organization and full completion of their journal. This helps provide the necessary individual accountability in a group environment.[xli]

2. **Analysis/Score by Faculty Instructor:** At the conclusion of the experiential learning course, students should submit their completed journal to the instructor. Using a rubric designed to measure the learning that has occurred during the course; the instructor analyzes and scores the journal content. This score should not be used in the final grading for the course. Rather, it is recommended that the journal component of a final grade be based upon the organization, effort and full completion of the specified requirements for the journal. Here, the rubric score provides a mechanism to demonstrate that learning has occurred.

Proposed Learning Goals for Course/Program

This initial step establishes the foundational areas for which assurance of individual learning must be provided. For our model, the learning goals for an experiential learning course that each student must meet are:

1. Demonstrate an understanding of the steps necessary to develop and facilitate a consulting project plan.
2. Demonstrate an understanding of the group collaborative process in decision making and project performance.
3. Recognize and conceptualize a complex issue into a clearly written summary.
4. Demonstrate an understanding of the organization's impact on the community.

The Purpose of Journal

This will be the tool used to determine if learning has occurred. Evaluation of responses to the same/similar questions asked at different points will provide data on learning progression. See Appendix 1B for an example of a Journal Requirements Outline to be provided to students. The journal should include the following:

1. **Standard Questionnaire** – Questions are designed to measure student's level of knowledge on relevant areas during various, pre-determined stages of the project. Relevant areas are derived from learning goals. It is important to note that the grade for the journal is based upon organization and effort to provide complete answers. The correctness of responses will not be part of the student's grade. This will allow students to respond honestly based upon the facts they have at that time. We recommend that the initial questionnaire, if possible, be administered in a classroom environment very early in the program. This will prevent students from doing further research to provide the "correct" answers. The goal of this initial survey is to establish a baseline measure of knowledge that the student brings into the program. If an in-person classroom survey is not possible or feasible, this could be done in an online test environment providing limited time for response and stating that outside resources should not be utilized, while emphasizing that the grade is not based upon accuracy of the answers. The same questionnaire should be given out 1-2 additional times during the project and at the end of the project. Further, review of these submissions can also provide feedback for faculty on areas which may require further communication or development, thus offering additional insight for learning experience improvements. See Appendix 1C for a sample Standard Questionnaire.

2. **Reflection**- Learning goal 4 invites the student to think about larger issues than those addressed directly in the project. Even though this technique originated in the service-learning environment, it is useful to all projects as it encourages critical thinking and

provides feedback on the relationship of the project to the wider world. Finally, the students' reflections on the final learning goal can be a source of future projects for the program, as well as yet another opportunity for the student to think creatively as an individual.

3. **Other Entries** –Throughout the program, the faculty instructor may add additional questionnaires or writing assignments as they feel needed or beneficial.

Rubric Use by Faculty Instructor

As determined by the school/instructor, the journal can be submitted intermittently throughout the project or only at the end of the project. We suggest three submissions. This will provide the faculty with two measures of progress and one final measure of learning. It will allow the faculty member to provide students with further guidance, information or requirements for journal entries during the remaining time to help achieve the learning goals. Alternatively, an online journal may be utilized.

A rubric should be used by the faculty member for the particular course or program in scoring the learning. Although not required, to add an additional level of objectivity, this analysis/scoring can also be done by an individual unconnected to the course such as another faculty member. The rubric must be completed with the learning goals clearly in mind. Appendix 2H provides a suggested rubric based upon the previously provided learning goals. An electronic tool for entering rubric data is highly recommended. This can be developed in Microsoft Excel or a similar program to allow faculty to enter scores while totals for each individual and overall statistics/reports for the class are automatically calculated. The development of a tool such as this will save significant time and can provide documentation of the process undertaken. In addition, it can provide the data needed for evaluation of program content and consideration of possible program improvements.

The rubric example (Appendix 2H) requires analysis and score of three variables for each learning goal. Data used for scoring will be obtained from journal entries including those submitted on behalf of the group (see Section 3 requirements on Appendix 1B). It is important to note that scores are to be given based upon individual performance and improvement which will include consideration of individual's impact on group's performance. Each variable will receive a score of 1-4. A score of "1" would reflect no ability or understanding/progress in this area.

The summary reflects a requirement of 48 overall points (with a minimum of 10 in any learning goal) as the minimum level required for successful attainment of learning goals. While the overall requirement requires a score that reflects an average at the level of "Accomplished", scoring at the "Accomplished" level is not required for each individual area. The rationale is that exemplary success in some variables with a developing success in other areas would document reasonable overall assurance of learning for learning goals. A score of 48 would not be required until the end of the program. Scores for the interim review(s) are anticipated to be in the "developing" range. Faculty should pay particular attention to areas which are not showing desired progress at interim reviews.

Utilizing Journals and Data for Future Program Development

Faculty should review scores as each program is completed. Any learning goal with an overall student average of under 12 would indicate a need for program improvement. Faculty should review the program to determine steps necessary to improve its content to a level where students will be able to master the variables.

Further, the journals can also be used to demonstrate to deans and chairs the efficacy of these projects. Feedback from stakeholders to administration can be one of the many benefits of these projects. Other benefits include measurement of learning objectives, and the creation of ideas for the future.[xlii]

APPENDIX ONE- TOOLS

Appendix 1A:

Question Areas for Analysis

Possible Threat (T) question areas:
- Economy
- Barriers to market entry
- Off-shore competition
- Demographic trends
- Regulatory environment
- Product or market life cycles
- Industry trends

Possible Opportunity (O) question areas:
- New products, markets, segments
- Diversification
- Technology
- Demographic trends
- Globalization
- Collaboration partners

Possible Weaknesses (W) question areas:
- Cost structure
- Capital
- Managerial skills
- New product development capability
- Marketing capacity
- Strategic alignment of initiatives
- Critical mass of products, sales, customers

Possible Strengths (S) question areas:
- Core competence
- Strategic plan
- Financial resources
- Profitability
- Business model
- Technology
- Marketing prowess
- Management team

Appendix 1B: Journal Requirements

Students are required to create and maintain a journal during the performance of this project. While online submission may be required for select assignments throughout the semester, a complete printed version of the journal will be required at the completion of the project. Exact dates provided in class calendar.

Journals will be graded based upon organization of journal and effort to provide complete responses/entries based upon level of knowledge at point of completion. The accuracy of responses will not be graded.

Journal requirements are as follows: Sections 1 and 2 must be submitted by each student. One copy of Section 3 is required per group.

Submitted individually by student:

Section 1: Standard Questionnaires – Completion of these questionnaires will be required throughout the program per the class schedule. This section should include copies of all questionnaires completed and submitted. These questionnaires are intended to be completed with 30 minutes or less without the use of other materials or resources. While some of the questions remain the same for each questionnaire, variation in the responses is anticipated as the student's experience grows and more information becomes available during the consulting assignment.

Section 2: Other Entries – Throughout the project, other questionnaires or written assignments may be requested by the Instructor. This section should include copies of these assignments as originally submitted.

Submitted by group:

Section 3: Project Materials – Copies of the following are required:
1. First draft of the Letter of Engagement
2. The final Letter of Engagement
3. The initial presentation to clients on overview of project
4. The final presentation to clients on results of project
5. The final report to clients
6. Any other deliverables provided to clients

Appendix 1C: Standard Questionnaire

Requirements: *(unless noted, responses should be no more than 1-3 paragraphs)*

First Submission: Responses to Section A only (limited to 30 minutes)

Interim Submissions: Responses to Sections A and B

Final Submission: Responses to Sections A, B and C

Section A:

1. Describe the purpose of a Letter of Engagement. Based upon your current knowledge, what do you believe it should include? Discuss what you see to be the main challenges in the development of a Letter of Engagement.
2. What do you see as the main issues to be addressed in designing the scope of a project and a project plan? What do you feel will create the largest challenges in staying within this scope?
3. Describe the challenges you anticipate (or have encountered) in working as part of a team consulting group who is addressing the needs of a client.
4. Describe the challenges you anticipate (or have encountered) in communicating and working with the assigned client. (If this is not the first questionnaire, please describe one communication issue which has occurred and what your group has done to address it. Also, describe how you feel you individually contributed to this resolution.)

Section B:

1. Explain the challenge (as you see it at this time) that your client has requested your group's assistance with.
2. At this point, what do you feel your group could have outlined better in the Letter of Engagement?
3. What improvements do you feel your group could have made in the initial communications with the client?
4. What is the largest challenge your group has experienced and how was it addressed or is being addressed?
5. To date, what do you feel is the most important thing you have learned during the performance of this project?

Section C:

1. Provide a 1 page summary of the challenge your client faced and how it was addressed by your group. Please include details on how you feel your group dynamics contributed to (or diminished) the success of your project.
2. What are the three most valuable things you learned during the completion of this assignment?
3. How might this learning experience be relevant to your future professional career?
4. How do you feel your learning experience in this program could have been improved?

APPENDIX TWO- TEMPLATES

Appendix 2A:

**STANDARD SURVEY COVER LETTER AND
SURVEY INSTRUMENT PREAMBLE**

(TO BE USED IN BOTH CIRCUMSTANCES)

We are a group of students in the Team Consulting Program at *insert school* conducting a survey for the benefit of *insert client's name*. If you have any questions about the survey, please contact the team leader, *insert team leader's name*, at *insert team leader's phone and/or email address*. If you have any questions about the Team Consulting Program, please contact the Director, *insert name* at insert phone number or insert email.

Appendix 2A:

Confidentiality and Participation Agreement

In consideration of my being selected for and being permitted to participate in a project that provides advice and assistance to small businesses, and thus receiving the increased educational experience that will result from my participation, I agree to the following:

1. I agree that I will treat in strict and absolute confidence all information received by me under this project. The only exception of this commitment will be other members of the Project Team and_____, who will supervise the project.
2. I agree that I will not recommend to the client any purchase of goods or services from sources in which I or other members of the Project Team may have an interest, nor will I accept fees, commissions, gratuities or other benefits from any firm or individuals that I may recommend to the client.
3. I certify that I am not now involved in a business that competes with my client and will not be involved in such a business during and immediately following the consultation. I hereby agree that I have no rights to compensation for any client improvements resulting from the work in this project.
4. I will maintain confidentiality of any client information permanently. I will never use or discuss any client information except with the Project Team during the consulting engagement.
5. I certify that neither myself nor any immediate family member has any interest in the ownership of the client's business.

_____	_____
Date	Consultant
_____	_____
Date	Consultant
_____	_____
Date	Consultant
_____	_____
Date	Consultant

Appendix 2B:

Student Background Information

Name-_____

Current Address-　　　_____

　　　　　　　　　　　_____

Phone: -　　　Home:_____　　　Cell: _____

E-Mail: School _____　　　Permanent _____

Student Status:
　　　Part Time ____ or Full Time ____
　　　Graduate ____ or Undergrad ____
　　　GPA _____

If Undergrad:　Year in program _____, Major _____-

If Graduate:
　　　Undergraduate Institution:_____
　　　Year of Graduation:　_____
　　　Major:　　　　　　　　_____

Work Experience (2 most recent positions, if applicable):

Employer/Title/Dates:_____
Responsibilities:　　_____
　　　　　　　　　　_____

Employer/Title/Dates:_____
Responsibilities:　　_____
　　　　　　　　　　_____

Professional Affiliations (if any):

_____
_____

(Appendix 2B - cont.)

Special Interests/Hobbies/Skills:_____

_____
_____
_____

Awards and Honors: _____

_____
_____
_____

Additional Languages:

Some Understanding		
Some Translation		
Fluent Translation/written		
Fluent Translation/ speech		

Other (please list any other attributes not mentioned that you think would be important to your consulting role): _____

_____
_____
_____

Appendix 2C: Company Contact Sheet

COMPANY: _____   SECTION: _____

COMPANY CONTACT(S):

NAME	TELEPHONE #	FAX NUMBER	E-MAIL

FACULTY ADVISOR: _____

TEAM MEMBERS:

NAME	HOME #	BUSINESS #	FAX NUMBER	E-MAIL ADDRESS

*Team Leader

Appendix 2D: Activity Log

Please log the total hours dedicated to the report. Round to the nearest quarter hour and use the following numbering system:

15 minutes = .25   30 minutes = .50   45 minutes = .75   1 hour = 1.00

Week	Discussion & Planning	Meeting with Client	Telephone/ Email Client	Research	Writing & Editing	Travel	Presentation	Other	TOTAL
1									
2									
3									
4									
5									
6									
7									
8									
9									
10									
11									
12									
13									
14									
15									

Appendix 2E: Team Progress Report

(submit 1 per team)

Team name_____ Date:_____

INTERVIEWS:

Name of firm_____ Person interviewed_____

Type of interview: at firm____ telephone____ other _____

Group members present/involved: _____

1) Purpose of interview (goals):

2) Information obtained:

TEAM ACTIVITY (not the interview)**:**

1) Describe any work done this week(s) related to the project:

2) Indicate the sources used in any research that was done:

3) Describe any problem areas you have encountered associated with the project. Have they been successfully overcome?

(Appendix 2E - cont.)

INDIVIDUAL ACTIVITY (each team member should list his/her name and what they did during this reporting period involving their consulting project):

1) _____

2)_____

3)_____

4)_____

Appendix 2F: Peer Evaluation Form

This is an anonymous evaluation. Be open, fair and constructive as you rate each team member **and yourself**. Use a 10-point rating scale, with 10 = superior and 1 = very weak.

Place names in column headings, and totals at bottom of each column.

If you'd like to add any comments, you may do so on the bottom of this form or attach a separate page.

When completed, please email it to _____or drop it off at _____.

This is due by _____ and counts towards your participation score. Thank you.

Names				
On time for all group meetings				
Helped keep the group cohesive				
Contributed number of useful ideas				
Quantity of work done				
Quality of work done				
Totals				

Appendix 2F: Client Evaluation Form

Client: _____ Term: _____

Please rate the performance of the Student Consulting team on your project.

Each area should be evaluated on a scale of 1-5, with 1 = poor and 5 = excellent.

Please return completed form to _____ via email _____ or
fax _____. Thank you.

			PERFORMANCE APPRAISAL
1.	Ability to understand the business environment and identify key issues		1 2 3 4 5
2.	Communication between client and consulting team		1 2 3 4 5
3.	Creativity		1 2 3 4 5
4.	Quality of analysis		1 2 3 4 5
5.	Quality of written reports		1 2 3 4 5
6.	Quality of presentations		1 2 3 4 5
7.	Follow through on proposed work plan		1 2 3 4 5
8.	Ability to synthesize current events and trends in the business world into the consulting work		1 2 3 4 5
9.	Overall professionalism of the consulting team		1 2 3 4 5
10.	Overall effectiveness of the consulting team		1 2 3 4 5

Comments:

Appendix 2G: CLIENT IMPACT SURVEY
(All information will be kept confidential)

1. In what semester did you receive SBI consulting? _____

2. In what year did you open/acquire your business?

    _____

3. How many full-time employees do you currently have?

    _____

    Part-time? _____

4. What is your total sales in your last fiscal year?

    $_____

5. Before working with the SBI program, would you describe your annual sales as:

    Growing _____
    Stable/flat _____
    Declining _____

    If growing or declining, by what percentage? _____?

6. How would you rate the knowledge and expertise of the SBI consultant team assigned to you?

    Excellent   Average   Poor
    1   2   3   4   5   6   7

7. After you received the consulting, do you plan to make any changes (or have you) in your business operations?

    _____Yes
    _____No

8. If "yes" to question 7, check all the appropriate areas where changes will occur (or have occurred)
    _____Business organization
    _____Sales/merchandising
    _____Advertising/promotion
    _____Accounting/bookkeeping
    _____Inventory control
    _____Business/strategic planning
    _____Financial analysis/statements
    _____Personnel policies
    _____Computers/info systems
    _____Other (Specify)_____

    _____
    _____

9. What is your estimate of potential savings/gains (either in decreased costs or enhanced revenues) resulting from the efforts of the SBI consultants?

_____

10. Can you describe a specific recommendation that the student team made that you followed, and its results to date?

_____

_____

_____

_____

_____

_____

11. Would you recommend that other organizations contact the SBI?

    • Yes   • No   • Uncertain

12. Do you have any additional comments you would like to make regarding your SBI experience with

_____

_____

_____

_____

_____

_____

_____

Name _____   Business Name _____

Address: _____   Phone Number_____

May we use your experiences with the SBI to promote the program? Yes ☐ No ☐   (any strategic/financial information would **not** be used)

Appendix 2H: Rubric

For use in evaluation of student journals.

Requirements: *(unless noted responses should be no more than 1-3 paragraphs)*
Student journals should be scored in each of the following categories. Total should be recorded for each subcategory.

Learning Goals:
1. Demonstrate an understanding of the steps necessary to develop and facilitate a consulting project plan.
2. Demonstrate an understanding of the group collaborative process in decision making and project performance.
3. Recognize and conceptualize a complex issue into a clearly written summary.
4. Demonstrate an understanding of the organization's impact on the community.

Learning	Concept:	Beginning 1	Developing 2	Accomplished 3	Exemplary 4	Score:
Goal: 1	Understands process of developing Letter of Engagement.	Demonstrates minimal knowledge.	Demonstrates awareness of need for LOE and steps necessary to prepare.	Understands the process necessary to develop a LOE	Demonstrates extensive insight on process. Thoroughly understands consequences of poorly developed LOE.	
	Understands process of developing project plan.	Demonstrates minimal knowledge.	Demonstrates expanding understanding.	Understands the process necessary to develop a project plan.	Identifies high level of knowledge on effective project development.	
	Understands process of developing and maintaining the scope for project.	Demonstrates minimal knowledge.	Demonstrates expanding understanding.	Demonstrates a thorough understanding on managing the scope of a project.	Is able to provide extensive insight on managing scope and has developed unique methods to do so.	
	Journal entries document an expanding understanding of project management.	Demonstrates minimal increased knowledge from initial entry.	Demonstrates some expanded understanding.	Clearly demonstrates an expanded level of understanding in this area.	Demonstrates a very high expansion of knowledge since initial entry.	
						Enter Score 1
					Total:	

2				Enter Score 2
Understands steps necessary for developing and maintaining successful group interactions.	Demonstrates minimal knowledge.	Demonstrates expanding understanding group dynamics.	Entries demonstrate a good understanding of group dynamics and how to be an effective member of a team.	Entries demonstrate an ability to identify potential problems and lead group to successful resolution of outstanding issues.
Journal entries document the attitude of an effective team player.	Demonstrates limited ability to interact as part of a group.	Entries reflect some participation in group including taking responsibility for assignments.	Entries reflect active participation in group, volunteering for assignments, meeting deadlines, etc.	Entries reflect strong participation and successfully assuming a role in some form of leadership position.
Journal entries reflect attitude of shared responsibility for team's results.	Demonstrates limited ability to see oneself as responsible for group's success.	Entries reflect understanding of need for commitment to the group and group's deadlines.	Entries reflect a strong commitment to the group's success.	Entries reflect an expanded organizational role in group's success.
Journal entries document an expanding understanding of the group collaborative process.	Demonstrates minimal increased knowledge from initial entry.	Demonstrates some expanded understanding.	Clearly demonstrates an expanded level of understanding in this area.	Demonstrates a very high expansion of knowledge since initial entry.
				Total:

3					Enter Score 3
Journal includes entries fully covering and detailing all required topics.	Entries do not fully cover many required topics.	Entries fully cover most required topics.	Entries fully cover the required topics.	Entries fully cover all required topics, are well organized and include additional detail and insight.	
Journal entries demonstrate an ability to effectively and concisely summarize the relevant, complex issues.	Entries lack organization and are difficult to understand.	Entries reflect some organization and effective summarization.	Entries include an effective and concise description of relevant and complex issues.	Entries and thoughts are extremely well organized demonstrating a very effective ability to identify and summarize all issues.	
Journal entries demonstrate an ability to recognize issues which may impact a project's success.	Entries reflect limited ability to identify relevant issues.	Entries reflect an expanding ability to recognize relevant issues.	Entries reflect an ability to recognize issues which will impact a project's success.	Entries reflect an ability to recognize issues as well as an ability to develop well thought out plans to address these issues.	
Journal entries demonstrate an increased ability to identify and conceptualize the issues impacting the project performance.	Demonstrates minimal increased knowledge from initial entry.	Demonstrates some expanded understanding.	Clearly demonstrates an expanded level of understanding in this area.	Demonstrates a very high expansion of knowledge since initial entry.	
				Total:	

4	Demonstrates minimal knowledge.	Demonstrates some understanding of the qualities of a community.	Is able to clearly define and describe a community.	Is able to define a complex web within a community.	Enter Score 4
Understands process of defining communities.					
Understands process of defining the communities' impact on the client.	Demonstrates minimal knowledge.	Demonstrates some expanded understanding of a possible impact.	Clearly demonstrates an understanding of more than one effect on the client.	Demonstrates a thorough knowledge of all the areas of impact on the client from the community.	
Journal entries demonstrate an ability to effectively and concisely summarize the relevant, complex issues.	Demonstrates minimal knowledge.	Demonstrates some expanded understanding of at least one issue.	Demonstrates an understanding of several issues.	Demonstrates knowledge of all the major issues.	
Journal entries demonstrate an increased ability to identify and conceptualize the client's impact on the community.	Demonstrates minimal knowledge.	Demonstrates an understanding of one effect on the community.	Clearly demonstrates an expanded level of understanding multiple effects and interactions.	Demonstrates a very high level of understanding of the role of the client in the community.	
				Total:	

Summary:

Learning Goal 1 Score: ____

Learning Goal 2 Score: ____

Learning Goal 3 Score: ____

Learning Goal 4 Score: ____

Total Score: ____

Met minimum level: Yes ____ No ____

(Requires total score of 48 with no individual learning goal falling below 10)

APPENDIX THREE: EXAMPLES

Appendix 3A: Sample Letters of Engagement

KJP Consulting
Student Consulting Team
Rider University

February 13, 2011

Mr. Daniel Josephs, I.C.E.
Spruce Industries, Inc.
759 E. Lincoln Avenue
Rahway, NJ 07065

Subject: Letter of Engagement between Spruce Industries, Inc and KJP Consulting (The Student Consulting Team)

We are delighted to have the opportunity to work with Spruce Industries, Inc. ("you" or "Client"). This letter of engagement describes the services to be performed and the relevant terms and conditions governing the relationship between us.

I.   Background

Hank Josephs purchased Spruce Industries, Inc. over 20 years ago. Hank's son Dan Josephs joined the business approximately five years ago to assist with the day to day operations of the business. Spruce Industries is a producer and distributor of sanitary cleaners, chemicals, and equipment offering complete sanitary solutions.

A few years ago Hank and Dan recognized an early trend in the marketplace. They realized that more people wanted cleaning solutions that were green. "Green" in the sanitary industry means chemicals that are non-toxic and/or products that have minimum impact on the environment. In the past, green cleaning products were not in as much demand because they often did not clean as well as traditional cleaning products and cost more. However, with developments in green cleaning chemistry, green products now clean equally well at the same price. Spruce's customer base consists of schools (45%), healthcare (10 – 15%), housing authorities (10 – 15%) with the balance consisting of different kinds of accounts such as airport terminals.

Spruce Industries is seeking the services of KJP Consulting to provide marketing recommendations to tap into the same consumer market. In connection with this engagement, the Student Consulting Team has referred to and relied upon information provided by Spruce Industries.

II. Project Objectives

Spruce currently sells and distributes cleaning products to businesses or organizations that use the products purchased for industrial purposes. With intense competition in this market, including product price cutting due to the recession, it is becoming increasingly difficult for Spruce to discover new business opportunities. Spruce would like KJP Consulting to make strategic business recommendations to effectively tap into the consumer market, specifically for their in-house (private label) and eco-friendly cleaning supplies.

To accomplish that objective, Spruce is looking to expand the consumer market through retail outlets. While this has never been attempted by Spruce, KJP Consulting will research if there is a significant opportunity to grow the revenue of the firm by obtaining shelf-space in retail outlets is feasible. In addition, Spruce would also like the Student Consulting Team to provide insightful ways to use the just-developed consumer website to meet his goal.

In order to develop a plan that will reach this market, the Student Consulting Team will conduct research with consumers and retailers to create a marketable brand of eco-friendly cleaning products that will appeal to the consumer market. This will entail creating a new brand name, and designing new packaging.

III. Approach

In order to meet the objectives of this project, KJP will conduct primary research that looks at retailers of eco-friendly products and how the products they carry are marketed and priced. The consulting team will evaluate the strengths and weaknesses of competitors to help determine what, if any, possible openings or competitive advantages are in the existing market. Part of this analysis will focus on process and its potential to create an advantage. For example, one competitive advantage that Spruce's private label eco-friendly brand products could have over some other consumer-based products is the necessary "green" certifications. Once this research is completed, a brand needs to be created that is appealing to the consumer in terms of product use, brand name, and packaging. Misco Product Corporation will be the source that will provide valuable information on private label branding and packaging to KJP Consulting. Five possible brand names that the consulting team has created will be surveyed in the consumer market using the services of Survey Monkey, an online survey website, to get a sample size of approximately 100 consumers. Based on the popularity of the brand names, they will be narrowed down and then the consulting team will make the final decision on which name to utilize.

While Spruce's eco-friendly consumer brand is being developed, primary research will be performed concurrently to determine the processes involved and feasibility in obtaining shelf space at various regional and/or local retailers. This primary research will consist of directly contacting two big box retailers (Target and Wal-Mart), two supermarkets (Wegman's and Whole Foods) and two environmentally conscious retail stores (located in New Hope, Pennsylvania area) through phone, email and onsite visits to obtain as much information as possible concerning the feasibility of obtaining shelf-space at these locations. Using this information, a plan will then be put together for Spruce's sales representatives to help them obtain accounts in the retail market.

Ultimately, KJP Consulting will make a recommendation to Spruce Industries as to whether or not it is feasible for Spruce Industries to enter the consumer market through this channel. Consistent with this recommendation we will also provide ideas towards the most effective use of existing consumer website.

IV. Client Deliverables

1. KJP Consulting will submit and formally present the project data to Spruce Industries in presentation form on or before April 10, 2011 (or a mutually acceptable date) at Rider University.
2. At the time of the presentation, Spruce Industries will receive a bound copy of the project containing the primary data, the secondary data, and the final recommendations of the Student Consulting Team.
3. Spruce Industries will have a new eco-friendly brand for household cleaning products regardless if the final decision is to recommend that Spruce pursue the consumer market.
4. Spruce Industries will be provided with a list of feasible retailers to target based on the primary research conducted by KJP, as well as a brochure that clearly defines the brand, brand slogan, and brand image to be utilized by Spruce's sales force.

V. Scope of Consulting Project/Responsibilities

General Guidelines

- Objectives and assumptions contained in the project proposal are based on information provided by Mr. Dan Josephs of Spruce Industries to the Student Consulting Team. Other assumptions may be made based upon the information that we receive during the site visit of Misco Products Corporation.
- This letter of Engagement will define the scope of the consulting project.
- Any modifications to project requirements must be agreed to by Mr. Joseph's, the Student Consulting Team and the professor. These modifications must be documented via e-mail or written agreement.

Spruce Industries Responsibilities

- Communicate project requirements openly and precisely. Dan Josephs will be the primary firm contact for KJP. Actively engage in product design and implementation.
- Commit the time and resources necessary to provide all requested information, feedback, and guidance on a timely basis.
- Be available to the Student Consulting Team at mutually agreeable times and locations, either via telephone or in person.
- Provide any resources and/or budget to the Student Consulting Team as agreed upon by this Letter of Engagement and in subsequent written authorization.

KJP Consulting Responsibilities

- Actively participate in all meetings to understand Spruce's requirements and deliverables.
- Remain in regular contact with Mr. Dan Josephs throughout the project. For simplicity, the majority of communication will take place through Kevin Lawton who represents KJP Consulting as a primary point of contact for Spruce Industries.
- Communicate project requirements openly and precisely.
- Manage project deliverables and timelines.
- Conduct all meetings and exchanges in a professional and courteous manner.
- Maintain the confidentiality of project information.
- Identify a single primary point of contact and supply additional contact information of all team members.

VI. Project Budget

At this stage in the process, no expenses are expected. Should expenses arise during the course of this project, they will require prior authorization by Mr. Dan Josephs. Authorization may be in the form of e-mail.

VII. Project Schedule

- Initial meeting will be held with Mr. Dan Josephs at Spruce Industries' Rahway NJ office to obtain information about the organization and its needs. This initial meeting was held on Monday, January 10, 2011.
- The second in-person meeting took place on February 15, 2011 at Misco Products Corporation in Reading, PA with Mr. Daniel Josephs. The purpose of this meeting was to better understand the different possibilities for redesigning the green private label product line for Spruce. During this meeting the Student Consulting Team examined possible products, ideas of making these products more eco-friendly and appearance of physical product through its packaging.
- Letter of Engagement will be completed by Thursday, March 3, 2011 and sent to Mr. Dan Josephs for his signature.
- Brainstorming will be done for finalized product line which will be done in collaboration with Mr. Dan Josephs, and will be done by the end of March.
- Research will be done in order to determine where Spruce may have a potential consumer market in the local area. This research will lead to the feasibility aspect of the plan and allow for a further understanding of which retail locations are best suited for the new product line. The research portion of this section will be completed by March 27, 2011.

Certain steps outlined above will be done concurrently. Project milestones will be marked with interim updates to Mr. Dan Josephs of Spruce Industries.

VIII. Agreement

The analysis, recommendations, and final report that will be provided should not be interpreted as the official position of Rider University or its staff. Rather, it will contain the views and opinions of the Small Business Institute's Student Consulting Team based on discussions, observations, investigations, and analysis of Spruce Industries operations and its business environment.

If circumstances arise that are beyond the control of the Student Consulting Team or Spruce Industries, and the completion of this project cannot be achieved, the Student Consulting Team and Spruce Industries shall jointly take a course of action that is mutually agreeable.

IX. Approval Signatures

(signatures on the copy that went to the client)

Appendix 3A

RUTGERS UNIVERSITY - Letter of Engagement

This letter of engagement is entered into between:

Rutgers Business School Consulting Team ("Consulting Team") 300 Ackerson Building, 180 University Avenue, Newark, NJ 07102 and **The Community Food Bank of New Jersey** ("FoodBank") 31 Evans Terminal Road, Hillside, NJ 07205.

I. Background

The FoodBank has retained the services of the Consulting Team to evaluate the feasibility of a for-profit venture utilizing donated raw materials received from XXX to create a bread based product for sale in XXX stores. The products under consideration include bread crumbs, croutons, and bread pudding mixes. The product would utilize the "Grains for Good" brand. The venture is designed to provide income to support FoodBank's non-profit operations and potentially provide employment to community members.

II. Key Contacts

For the Consulting Team: XXX, Team Leader, XXXX
For FoodBank: XXX Project Manager, XXXXX

III. Team Membership (removed for confidentiality)

IV. Scope

The project will focus on one of the three bread products determined to be most viable and will conduct a comprehensive assessment of this product to fully gauge its feasibility. The project will only consider production in-house at FoodBank and will respect an initial investment cap of $10-15K. The Consulting Team will leverage its strengths in finance, marketing and operations to calculate a financial break-even analysis, create a marketing plan proposal, and conduct a preliminary supply chain analysis. Additionally, the project will include information gathering regarding the legal and regulatory environment surrounding the launch of a food product but will not include a formal analysis. With the understanding that this is a limited time engagement, the Consulting Team will outline suggested steps for moving forward with the project after the end of the engagement.

V. Deliverables

The Consulting Team will deliver and present their findings in the form of a written report and PowerPoint presentation on December 14, 2007. The report will include:

- Market analysis
- Product and packaging analysis and recommendation
- Financial analysis
- Logistics/Production analysis
- Promotion plan proposal
- Risk factor analysis
- Preliminary legal and regulatory information gathering
- Next Steps

VI. Responsibilities

General Guidelines
- Objectives and assumptions contained in the project proposal are based on information provided by Client to the Consulting Team.
- Formal project meetings will be held between members of the Consulting Team and the Client as provided in the project timeline.
- This Letter of Engagement will define the scope of the consulting project.
- Any modifications to project requirements must be agreed to by both the Client and the Consulting Team and must be documented via e-mail or written agreement.

Consulting Team
- Actively participate in all meetings to understand FoodBank's requirements and deliverables.
- Remain in regular contact with Mr. XXX throughout the project.
- Communicate project requirements openly and precisely.
- Manage project to submit deliverables on time.
- Conduct all meetings in a professional and courteous manner.

Client Responsibilities
- Communicate requirements openly and precisely.
- Actively engage in project design and implementation.
- Communicate and agree upon the scope of the project and deliverables.
- Commit the time and resources necessary to provide all requested information, feedback, and guidance on a timely basis.
- Be available to the Consulting Team at mutually agreeable times and locations, either via telephone or in person.
- Provide any resources and/or budget to the Consulting Team as agreed upon by this Letter of Engagement and in subsequent written authorizations.
- Identify a single primary point of contact. Currently, XXX is identified as the primary point of contact.

VII. Meeting Schedule

Task	Start Date	Milestone Date
Signed Letter of Engagement		23-Oct-2007
Marketing Analysis	25-Sept-2007	
Competition		14-Oct-2007
Product/packing analysis		30-Oct-2007
Promotion Proposal		12-Nov-2007
Logistics/Production Analysis	15-Nov-2007	
Risk Assessment		30-Nov-2007
Financial Assessment	30-Nov-2007	5-Dec-2007
Next Steps	5-Dec- 2007	10-Dec-2007
Final Presentation		14- Dec-2007

VIII. Fees &Budget

The payment of consulting fees is outside the scope of this Letter and is between Rutgers University and FoodBank. The Consulting Team may incur expenses such as travel mileage, parking costs, printing costs, etc.. No costs will be incurred without the written pre- approval of FoodBank and at no time will total costs exceed $500.

IX. Entire Agreement

This Letter of Engagement is the complete and only agreement between the two parties (excluding the aforementioned consulting fees) and any modification to the letter must be made in writing or electronic mail and agreed to by both parties.

The analysis, recommendations, and final report that will be delivered should not be interpreted as the official position of Rutgers University or its staff. The deliverables contain the views and opinions of the Consulting Team based on discussions, observations, investigations, research and analysis of FoodBank's operations and business environment.

If circumstances arise that are beyond the control of the FoodBank or the Consulting Team which inhibit the completion of the project, the parties shall jointly take a course of action that is mutually agreeable.

X. Signatures (removed for confidentially)

Appendix 3B: Sample Consulting Reports

Clean With The Power Of Green

Spruce Industries, Inc.

A Feasibility Study on Entering the Consumer Market
for "Green" Cleaning Products

Spring 2011

Rider University Student Consulting Team:
Xxx
Xxx
Xxx

(Under the direction of Professor Dr. Ronald Cook,
Director of Entrepreneurial Studies & the Small Business Institute® at Rider University)

(This report is included to enhance the learning experience for the student. It shows an excellent
example of a consulting project. The client has given permission for it to be used.)

Table of Contents

I. Executive Summary

Spruce Industries, Inc. is a janitorial supplies company located in Rahway, NJ. Janitorial supply companies are the largest segment within the overall industry known as the Service Establishment Equipment & Supplies Wholesaling, and make up 31% or $5.5 billion of the $18.5 billion total revenue that represents the industry. Providers of janitorial services purchase cleaning products in bulk from wholesalers like Spruce. In 2009, due to the recession, demand for janitorial services decreased which meant lower demand for cleaning supplies. The demand for cleaning supplies and equipment of the janitorial services industry was also affected by the increased vacancy rate of offices and other large facilities.

Janitorial supply companies will continue to face intense competition as customers continue to bypass wholesalers and purchase directly from the manufacturer (often overseas). While the recession has had its impact on the industry, new trends have emerged like the focus on "green" or eco-friendly cleaning products. Maintaining a competitive advantage in this industry continues to be based on pricing, quality, range of products, service and flexibility.

Industry demand is expected to see only modest growth in the short term. A significant and increasing proportion of this growth is expected to be represented by environmentally safe cleaners. One market research firm projects that sales in the "green" cleaning product market will triple by 2014 to $1.6 billion and more than double its share of household and laundry cleaning market. The term "green" is used to refer to products and processes that are safer for the environment. "Green" products are generally those that have reduced toxicity, biodegradability, and reduced and recyclable packaging.

The trend towards "green" products is increasing rapidly due to three factors. Eco-friendly cleaning products offer health and environmental benefits over the traditional products. "Green" cleaning products are also increasing in popularity because they are now considered to clean as well if not better than conventional products. Finally, the growing demand for these products has led to more cost-competitive pricing against traditional counterparts, making consumers more likely to give them a try.

The team project was aimed at assisting Spruce in penetrating the consumer market for "green" cleaning products. We provided Spruce with strategic business recommendations relating to private label branding and product line recommendations, the process and feasibility of obtaining retail shelf space, and website recommendations for Spruce's new consumer website. Our findings in these areas are summarized below, followed by our final recommendations for Spruce.

Strategic Business Recommendations
A. Consumer Survey Results
> 1.) The market for eco-friendly cleaning products currently exists but even more significant are the amount of non-users that could become users in the future.

> 2.) The three most utilized household cleaning products are all-surface, bathroom and glass cleaner. Any private-label "green" product line should include these.

> 3.) The top three factors that influence cleaning product purchase decisions are brand, price and products that have "green"/eco-friendly attributes.

4.) We would not recommend that Spruce spend the extra money to reflect the EcoLogo certification on the cleaning products line labels.

B. Private Label Branding & Packaging

The team is recommending the use of ReThink Clean™ as the private-label brand for Spruce's "green" cleaning product line. (see label example in section VI.- c.)

C. Process & Feasibility of Obtaining Retail Shelf Space

1.) Tier 1 – National Retailers (Wal-Mart & Target): Firms carried only a few "green" cleaning products-low saturation. However, barriers to entry for a new product vendor are very prohibitive.

2.) Tier 2 – Regional Retailers (Wegmans & Whole Foods Market): Firms had slightly higher levels of "green" cleaning products than national stores. While ease of becoming a new vendor seemed more accessible, than Tier 1 stores, we found that it was still very difficult.

3.) Tier 3 – Local/Specialized Retailers (Big Bear Natural Foods & Whole Earth Center): Stores had extremely high levels of "green" cleaning products already on shelf. However, barriers to entry (accessibility towards becoming a new vendor) were extremely low.

D. Consumer Website Recommendations

1.) Change in the website name from Strictly Quarts to something that would allow the consumer to associate the products Spruce sells to the name (potentially ReThink Clean™ if this product line is pursued further).

2.) Change the "log-in" location to make it more visible to returning customers.

3.) Include educational material related to "green"/eco-friendly cleaning trends.

4.) Change (or completely remove) the location of the "MSDS" field, and alteration of the Resources feature.

5.) Change the overall color scheme from the current dark to brighter colors

Conclusion & Final Recommendations

If Spruce Industries has interest in pursuing the consumer cleaning product market at the retail store level, we would recommend that it target only Tier 3 Regional Retailers (Big Bear Natural Foods and/or Whole Earth Center) on a 6-12 month trial basis with the ReThink Clean™ brand. We would also recommend that Spruce consider developing/locating one or more retailers in the tri-state area that are smaller than the regional retailers we identified, but larger than the local retailers. In doing so, Spruce may consider the ReThink Clean™ product line trial basis with this retailer as well.

II. Business Description/Company History

History

Hank Josephs purchased Spruce Industries over twenty years ago. Hank's son, Dan Josephs, joined the business approximately three years ago to assist with the day-to-day operations of the business. Spruce Industries is a producer and distributor of sanitary cleaners, chemicals, and equipment, offering complete sanitary solutions. They currently sell to commercial/industrial customers.

A few years ago Hank and Dan recognized an early trend in the marketplace. They realized that more people wanted cleaning solutions that were green. "Green" in the sanitary industry means chemicals that are non-toxic and/or products that have minimum impact on the environment. Their focus since then has been to become a leader in the marketplace of green sanitary products.

Business Structure

Spruce is a regional business and delivers to customers in the tri-state area and beyond with customers in NY, NJ, PA and CT. Spruce's customers consist of schools (45%), healthcare (10-15%), housing authorities (10-15%) with the balance consisting of different kinds of accounts such as airport terminals.

Product

In addition to selling a wide range of janitorial supplies, Spruce offers a fluorescent bulb recycling program for its customers in which they pick up old bulbs, recycle them and then provide a recycling certificate to their clients. Currently, Spruce provides this service for 4 of its customers.

Recently, Spruce became a distributor of Philips products. Philips manufactures green lighting products. Over the past few years, more awareness has been building around the fact that incandescent and fluorescent lights are inefficient and emit more carbon that alternatives available today. California has recently passed mandates limiting the amount of mercury vapor that can be emitted from some lighting. As more and more businesses switch to greener lighting products, Spruce will be poised to supply many customers within their geographical selling area.

Staff

Spruce is a medium-sized business with approximately $5 million in annual sales. Those sales are generated by 4 full-time and 3 part-time sales people. The commission structure varies slightly among the sales staff. Spruce's other staff consist of 3-4 delivery drivers and 3-4 office staff.

Cost Structure

Spruce sells branded products such as Clorox and Rubbermaid. They also sell their own private label brand. Gross margins on branded products are approximately 25%, while gross margins on private label products are closer to 50%. The cost of delivering the product is 16-17%.

III. Project Description

The project is described in the Letter of Engagement as signed by Daniel Josephs and the Rider Student Consulting Team (see Appendix C). The Rider Student Consulting Team's goal for this project is to recommend a strategic plan for Spruce to enter the consumer market. Spruce currently sells industrial cleaning supplies to schools, healthcare establishments, housing authorities, etc.. Spruce's sales and profits over the last 20 years have continued to grow but as of late, the industrial market has become more competitive. The latest trend in industrial cleaning is the growth of "Green" cleaning products. Spruce has been thinking about possible ways to enter the consumer market to keep their sales and profits on a positive growth track. Towards this goal, Spruce developed a website called "Strictly Quarts" to target the consumer market but no additional steps have been taken on how to draw people to the website.

Following a meeting with the client, Daniel Josephs, and preliminary research about the market and product, the following objectives were determined. The student consulting team's responsibilities were to:

- Make strategic business recommendations to effectively tap into the consumer market for Spruce's private label and eco-friendly cleaning products.
- Conduct research with consumers and retailers to provide input on what consumers demand of an eco-friendly cleaning product.
- Create a marketable brand of eco-friendly cleaning products that will appeal to the consumer market.
- Provide suggestions on how to utilize the Strictly Quarts consumer website.

The initial portion of our strategic approach involved creating a consumer survey on the perceptions of "green" cleaning products. The results from this survey provided us with valuable information which served as the basis for our decisions about the popularity of different cleaning products, the importance of "green" certifications and other factors that influence consumer purchase decisions. Also, with the help of Misco Products Corporation (one of our client's valued business partners), we developed a private-label brand name and packaging for the "green" cleaning product line.

The next step involved gathering information related to the process involved and feasibility of obtaining shelf-space at the retail level. Before considering the process and actual feasibility however, it was important to consider the existing saturation of the retail market for "green" cleaning products. We gathered this information on a three-tiered approach including 2 retailers from each market space as follows: Tier 1 – National Retailers (including Wal-Mart and Target); Tier 2 – Regional Retailers (Wegmans & Whole Foods Market); and Tier 3 – (Big Bear Natural Foods and Whole Earth Center, located in central NJ/eastern PA areas).

Obtaining this information has allowed us to evaluate the potential feasibility and opportunity associated with obtaining retail shelf space as a means to access the consumer market.

IV. Industry Analysis

Industry Overview

Spruce Industries is part of the Service Establishment Equipment & Supplies Wholesaling in the US industry (NAICS code#42185). The industry consists of companies that sell specialized equipment and supplies used by service establishments. These products are further described as janitorial equipment, carpet and floor cleaning equipment, carpet sweepers, vacuuming systems, floor sanding equipment and mop wringers. The industry also includes the wholesaling of beauty parlor, barbershop products, and laundry and dry cleaning products and equipment (IBIS World, 2010). The industry analysis that follows will focus primarily on the janitorial equipment and supply wholesalers and, where possible, make every effort to exclude information/data that is not applicable to this sub-segment.

Revenue for the industry from 2009 to 2010 is expected to increase by 5.1% to $18.45 billion. Unfortunately this represents only a partial recovery from the fall in demand that was experienced as a result of the economic recession (IBIS World, 2010). As corporate profits were squeezed during the recession, so were the budgets of these corporations and institutions. As a result, businesses began cutting back spending where ever possible.

The largest market for this industry is Janitorial Services. The providers of these services purchase cleaning products in bulk from wholesalers in this industry. In 2009, revenues of companies within the Janitorial Services Industry declined 5.2%. The falling demand for janitorial services directly led to the falling demand of cleaning supplies that these companies purchase from wholesalers. The amount of cleaning supplies and equipment required by the janitorial and custodial service company's was also affected by the increased vacancy rate of offices, shopping centers and factories that occurred in the midst of the recession (IBIS World, 2010).

While industry demand is expected to improve from 2010 to 2011 as the economy continues to recover (by 2.1% to $18.84 billion), businesses in the industry will still have its challenges. It is expected that an increased number of clients will continue to bypass wholesalers and instead purchase equipment and supplies directly from the manufacturer. As more clients purchase products directly from manufacturers, the industry has experienced more and more consolidation. This has forced existing wholesalers to take part in price competition which reduces their profit margins (IBIS World, 2010). Also, while the economic recession had impacted this industry overall, new trends within the industry were beginning to emerge. Despite the impact of the economy, a 2009 report by Green Seal and Enviromedia Social Marketing revealed that 58% of consumers were buying green cleaning products. Also, 19% of the 1,000 people surveyed noted that they are actually buying more green products in 2009 than before the recession (Williamson, 2009).

The industry is characterized by a low level of globalization. Most operators are local or regional companies that operate within the United States and do not have the capacity to service a global client base. While the level of globalization is low, an increasing number of clients who have begun purchasing products directly from the manufacturer are doing so through manufacturers overseas (IBIS World, 2010).

Maintaining a competitive advantage in the industry continues to be based on three pillars (not in order of importance): First, the range and quality of products that a distributor sells is important because it allows the firm to supply and service a large number of clients. Competitive pricing is also important as many customers (especially commercial) can be very price sensitive. The recent recession has also increased the price elasticity of the industry's customer base. Finally, flexibility and service orientation of a company that operates in the industry is also critical (IBIS World, 2010). Out of the three mentioned above, this last may be considered the hallmark to seeking any kind of competitive advantage. If the firm does not carry the products a client wants, it will buy from someone else. Also, if a firm's prices are not within a reasonable range, a client will buy elsewhere. Therefore, the flexibility, responsiveness and service orientation (including relationship management) that a company offers seems to be what will differentiate them from their competitors.

Industry Outlook – "Green" Cleaning

The modest growth projected over the next five years is expected to come from trends in green cleaning, a process by which products are developed from sustainable raw materials and/or are non-toxic. The trend is being generated by increased awareness by the end user in the areas of health and wellness and in the well being of the environment. These increases will offset decreases in growth resulting from the recent poor economic conditions (Sanitary Maintenance Magazine/ISSA, 2007). The 2010 IBISWorld Industry Report points out that specialty cleaning products such as environmentally safe floor cleaners are expected to represent a growing proportion of wholesale purchases. A market research firm known as Packaged Facts projects that sales in the green cleaning product market will triple to over $1.6 billion by 2014. This constitutes approximately 8 percent of the total cleaning product market. They even believe that green cleaners will more than double their share of the household and laundry cleaner market (Fleenor, 2010).

In order to understand the importance of the trend towards "green" cleaning products, it is necessary to begin with a discussion of what makes a product green. While the definition of "green" may differ from company to company, the Environmental Protection Agency (EPA) offers some objectivity in its definition. Olive Davies of the EPA says the term green is used broadly to refer to products and processes that are better for the environment. For products deemed to be safer for the environment, the EPA allows them to carry the Design for the Environment (DfE) logo. The EPA has a DfE scientific review team that screens each ingredient for potential human health and environmental effects. In other words, it is a science-based product certification. Product manufacturers who are fortunate to receive the DfE designation have invested heavily in research and development in order to create a greener product, while maintaining or improving product performance (Garrison, 2009). In addition to the EPA's DfE designation, EcoLogo and Green Seal are the two other well-known "green" designations. Not only do these certification agencies certify certain green products, they also play a major role in educating consumers about their benefits (Fleenor, 2010). Both Green Seal and EcoLogo have similar certification processes in which products must meet minimum standards to be considered. Green Seal for example, has specific standards for household cleaning products, which includes product performance requirements and environmental and health requirements such as reduced toxicity, biodegradability, and reduced and recyclable packaging (Greenseal.org, 2011). The EcoLogo program compares products with others in the same category, develops rigorous and scientifically relevant criteria that reflect the entire lifecycle of the product, and awards the EcoLogo certification to those that are verified by an independent third party as complying with the criteria (Environmentalchoice.com, 2011).

The use of green cleaning products is increasing rapidly due to the health and environmental benefits they offer. At the end of 2004, one out of every three chemical cleaning products contained ingredients known to cause human health or environmental problems (Case, 2004). A 2009 Healthcare Purchasing News article states that conventional cleaning products are a major contributor to indoor air quality issues in closed environments. What's worse is that many cleaning products contain cancer-causing carcinogens and an estimated 35% of conventional cleaning products can cause blindness, severe skin damage, or damage to organs through the skin. Furthermore, some cleaning products even harm the environment by contaminating water and harming aquatic life (Williamson, 2009). As of 2004, the institutional cleaning industry used five billion pounds of chemical per year in creating their products (Case, 2004). It is for these reasons that many organizations and individuals are exploring alternatives to their traditional cleaning products.

Green cleaning products are also becoming more popular because they now clean as well if not better than conventional cleaning products. "In numerous independent laboratory tests conducted on behalf of a group of large purchasers, all of the safer products bought by the group work as well or better than traditional counterparts" (Chase, 2004 p. 15). Consumers are no longer skeptical of a green cleaners performance and as a result, are more willing to purchase a green cleaner.

In the past, consumers and institutions alike had a pay a premium for a green product. The growing demand in the industry for green cleaning products has led to more competitors, and as a result, has led to far more cost-competitive pricing (Williamson, 2009). Not only are green cleaning products effective, they are also affordable. Some government agencies have even achieved a cost savings by switching from traditional products to green products. Cost savings or not, many public purchasers report that greener cleaners are cost competitive.

V. SWOT Analysis of Spruce Industries

Strengths

As with the previous Rider Student Consulting Teams, we had difficulty finding areas needing great improvement, a testament to Spruce management. Their strengths include:

- Strong vendor relationships: Spruce has a relationship with one of its vendors that spans over 20 years. This vendor partners with Spruce in manufacturing and marketing their private label products.
- Unique selling proposition: Spruce offers its customers a wide breadth of products, quick turnaround time, low minimums and ancillary services such as fluorescent bulb recycling.
- Strong sales and operations organization: Spruce recently upgraded their point of sale software to be better able to service their customers. They also have a good sense of who they are as a company and what products and customers are their "sweet spot" in terms of profitability.
- Openness to learning and improving all aspects of the company.

Weaknesses

- Aging sales force: Most of Spruce's sales force are in the last 10 years of their career.
- Spruce buys from 85 different manufacturers. Because of this, not all of their products are featured on their on-line catalog nor do they have one single source from which to find an item. Although this is not the team's expertise, we do recognize that there is improvement that could be made in this area so that it is easier for a customer to find what they are looking for, order it online and be able to track their order.

Opportunities

- Pursuing the currently un-tapped consumer market
- Converting more of their existing customers from branded products to private label products.
- As Spruce looks to slowly incorporate a new sales staff, they will have the opportunity to make sure the new sales people more closely reflect their customers, in terms of demographics.
- A formal marketing plan that focuses on targeting different customer segments, executed on a regular basis could reap new customers for Spruce.

Threats

- There are currently a large number of competitors of cleaning products for both commercial and household use. Even with Spruce's focus "green" cleaning products, it is difficult for Spruce to compete in the commercial market and they will face strong competition in the consumer area if they enter it.
- The economy is squeezing many of Spruce's customers into reducing facilities staff and lowering costs. This puts pressure on Spruce's margins. Spruce needs to continue to add value to its customer relationships in order to retain them as they are not the lowest cost provider.
- If Spruce does not actively recruit new sales people, it runs the risk of losing customers as its sales staff exits the industry over the next few years.
- The size of the commercial market is not expanding, so Spruce is under constant competitive pressure. If a sales person leaves and takes a key account to another competitor, it could affect profitability.

VI.   Strategic Business Recommendations

Consumer Survey Results

The Student Consulting Team conducted primary research in the form of a consumer survey. The objective of creating and distributing the survey was to obtain information on the consumer perceptions of "green" or eco-friendly cleaning products to supplement the data we had already gathered through our secondary research. We were also interested in using the consumer feedback to assist in the development of a brand-name and image for packaging of the selected consumer products. The survey was distributed via email to colleagues, family members, and friends of the student consulting team. Participants were able to respond via an online survey format. For reference, a copy of the consumer survey has been included in Appendix A.

The survey results provided the student consulting team with feedback on 6 primary areas of interest: (1) the percentage of respondents who use "green"/eco-friendly cleaning products; (2) the highest utilized cleaning products; (3) factors influencing purchase decisions; (4) recall of "green" logos/certifications; and (5) the influence that "green" certifications have on purchase behavior. Overall, there were 100 respondents to the survey.

The pie chart below reflects that the majority of respondents (46%) do not currently use "green"/eco-friendly cleaning products. It was surprising to see however that 37% of respondents do currently use these products (the remaining 17% were not sure). As a result of these responses we can conclude that 1 in 3 respondents use "green" cleaners. The response to this question also tells us that 46% of respondents do not use "green" cleaning products at all. The market for eco-friendly cleaners exists (1 in 3 current consumers), but there is also potential for the non-users (46%) to become users of these products in the future.

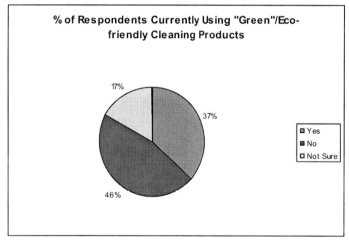

The response to the next question shown in the table below identifies the most popular and/or utilized type of cleaning products from a list that was provided to respondents. A usage rating of 1 represents most often and 5 represents least often. All-surface cleaner tends to be used the most among the list, followed by bathroom cleaner and then glass cleaner. The answer is important as we needed to determine what household cleaners are used the most in order to make product suggestions. These top three utilized cleaners will be the basis of the "green" consumer product line developed for Spruce Industries; all-surface, bathroom and glass.

Types of Cleaner Usage
(1 = most often, 5 = least often)

Type of Cleaner	Usage	Ranking
All Surface Cleaner	1.6	#1
Bathroom Cleaner	2.27	#2
Glass Cleaner	2.57	#3
Degreaser	3.96	#4
Other	4.28	#5

We also sought to gain a better perspective on the different factors that influence cleaning product purchase decisions. As one might expect, brand is the number one factor that influences the cleaning product that a consumer purchases. If this were not true, major manufacturers would not spend the time and money they do in developing their brand and increasing brand-awareness. Once we get past brand, consumers say that price is the next factor of importance, which means that Spruce needs to be conscious of the price it charges for this private label product. Furthermore, the survey results show that "green"/eco-friendly concept ranks third on the scale of factors that influence consumer purchase decisions of cleaning products. "Green"/eco-friendly products came in as more important to these respondents than product appearance (2.9 vs. 3.8).

**Factors that Influence Cleaning
Product Purchase Decisions**
(1 = high influence, 5 = low influence)

Factors	Rating	Ranking
Brand	1.9	#1
Price	2	#2
"Green" or Eco-Friendly	2.87	#3
Appearance of Product	3.82	#4
Other	4.28	#5

When designing the packaging for the "green" cleaning product line, we wanted to find out whether consumers are aware of and/or recognize the three most widely used logos or certifications (Green Seal, Design for Environment and EcoLogo). The results indicated that just under half of all respondents recognize one of the three logos shown in the survey, while more than half (56%) did not recognize any of these. If the survey results had shown that almost 44 percent of respondents (the sum of those who recognized at least one logo) recognized only one of the three logos, then that would be reason to consider reflecting that specific logo on the spray-bottle packaging. Since this did not occur and the majority of respondents did not recognize any logos, we concluded that it would not be cost-effective to pay the extra cost of $2,000 in addition to a one-time fee of $800 (per Misco) to have the rights to reflect the EcoLogo certification on the spray-bottle packaging. If in the near future these "green" certifications become more widely known amongst the general public this opinion may change.

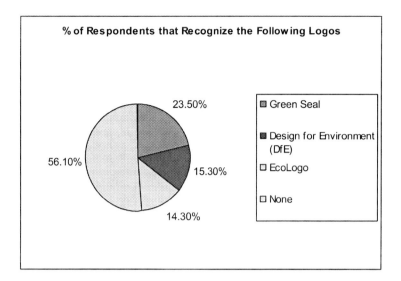

The question that follows asked participants what "green" logos/certifications (if any) would encourage you to purchase a cleaning product. Misco only has the ability to stamp their private-label products with the EcoLogo certification, so while 23.5% of respondents said that this logo would encourage them to purchase, it would again lead us to the same conclusion that it would not be worth it to pay to reflect this logo on the packaging. Also, about 41% of respondents still said that none of these certifications would encourage them to purchase a "green" cleaning product. Further, Peter Gable, Internal Sales Coordinator at Misco Products mentioned that there would not be a benefit in spending the additional money to have the EcoLogo reflected on the Spruce private-label consumer product line.

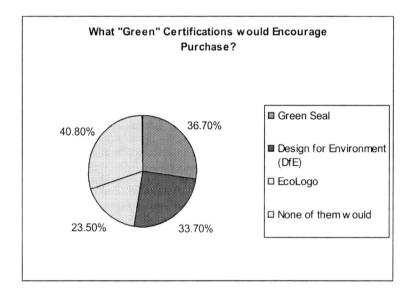

Private Label Branding & Packaging

In addition to providing some basic information related to the use of "green" cleaning products, the survey results served as the basis for our decisions about the cleaning products within the product line, the importance of "green" certifications and factors that influence consumer purchase decisions.

The student consulting team made the decision on the new brand name for the "green" cleaning product line. The team developed 10 potential names and then had several focus group discussions to come to an agreement on one of these. We wanted a brand name that would stand out to the consumer. Ultimately, we decided on the brand name ReThink Clean. We thought this brand name encompassed the certain connotations that we wanted this product line to have: simple, effective, powerful, forward-thinking, "green" cleaning.

After the product line had been determined and a brand name had been selected, the next step was designing the logo and packaging for the spray-bottle. Spruce Industries' partnership with Misco Products Corporation allows them access to Misco's Brandvantage program. This program allows Misco clients to develop a private label brand identity. As a result, the student consulting team worked directly with Misco's graphic designers to develop this brand image.

While the survey was being conducted, the student consulting team searched through the website Fotolia.com (recommended by Misco) for a potential stock photo that could be used in creating the brand image. Initially we selected approximately 25 stock images with "green"/nature/cleaning-related themes, and eventually narrowed it down to two images that contained industrial-like gear components (to represent the industrial strength of the product) coupled with earth and plant-like content (to represent the "green" aspect). Combining these two ideas came about from a very compelling suggestion that Joe Zhou (Vice President of Research & Development) raised during a discussion at our Misco site visit. As we discussed marketing this "green" consumer cleaning product line with Joe, he recommended that we that we consider the industrial background of Misco's private label "green" cleaning products as part of our marketing ploy.

Misco's eco-friendly product line is primarily used in a commercial and industrial cleaning capacity. This specific product line has a proven track record for reliability and working as well if not better than its traditional cleaning product counterparts. The idea is that if these eco-friendly products work well for industrial cleaning, they will certainly be effective for the consumer's cleaning needs.

Now that we had identified the brand name and chosen an image, we worked directly with one of Misco's graphic designers to pull it all together. Below is a graphic of the final spray-bottle packaging for the three products within the "green" cleaning consumer product line.

Process & Feasibility of Obtaining Retail Shelf Space

To develop this section, we first considered the "green" cleaning products that are already being sold by various retailers at the three main consumer retail distribution channels (National Stores/Tier 1, Regional Stores/Tier 2, and Local-Specialized Stores/Tier 3). This provided us with information about the potential competition and about the level of saturation of each retailers' "green" cleaning product category. Following a review of the existing "green" cleaning product lines of each store, we discuss the process that each store requires in order for a supplier to become a potential vendor.

Tier 1 – National Retailers

The largest holder of market share for consumer cleaning supplies is being sold by national "discount retailers". Wal-Mart is at the top of this list with 4,300 stores in the United States followed by Target with 1,755 stores in the United States. It makes logical sense to research how the largest national chains are merchandising their floors. These chains provide a general pulse on national consumer demand.

Wal-Mart

Existing "Green" Product Lines – Wal-Mart

Market research was conducted at the Wal-Mart in Princeton, New Jersey. This store carried three different brand-name "green"/eco-friendly cleaning products as follows: Clorox Green Works, Windex-Nature's Source, and Seventh Generation. The individual products behind these brand names include an all-purpose cleaner, glass cleaner, and bathroom cleaner. Below is a summary of Wal-Mart's cleaning products by brand name, price, and size; as of March 2011:

Clorox Green Works		
All-Purpose Cleaner	$2.97	32 fl. oz.
Windex-Nature's Source		
Glass Cleaner	$2.77	32 fl. oz.
Seventh Generation		
All Purpose Cleaner	$2.97	32 fl. oz.
Bathroom Cleaner	$2.97	32 fl. oz.

The Process of Becoming a Potential Vendor – Wal-Mart

Wal-Mart's process for becoming a cleaning supplies vendor is handled entirely through their website. Wal-Mart store managers are able to purchase locally produced products but nothing that contains chemicals. All buying decisions are made through their corporate office. On www.walmart.com, an online product submission must be completed. This entailed filling out the submission form, including the UPC, and a picture of the product. Once this first step is completed a D&B (Supplier Evaluation Report) is run at the vendor's expense. Supplier evaluation reports are used to judge the financial strength of a company. Wal-Mart will then let you know if they are interested in your product or not. As this was an investigation as to the purchase process, an actual D&B was not done. From here, if Wal-Mart is interested in your product you will still have to pass a number of hurdles in order to do business. Some of these include electronic data interchange, timely shipping, lead time requirements, product quality, transportation logistics, and security tagging.

Target

Existing "Green" Product Lines - Target

Market research was also conducted at the Target in Princeton, New Jersey. This store carried three different brand-name "green"/eco-friendly cleaning products as follows: Clorox Green Works, Seventh Generation, and Method. Method is a brand exclusive to Target. This means no other retailer can carry this line of products. The individual products behind these brand names include an all-purpose cleaner, glass cleaner, and bathroom cleaner. Below is a summary of Target's cleaning products by brand name, price, and size; as of March 2011:

Clorox Green Works

All Purpose Cleaner	$2.79	32 fl. oz.

Method

All Purpose Cleaner	$2.99	32 fl. oz.

Seventh Generation

All Purpose Cleaner	$2.99	32 fl. oz.
Bathroom Cleaner	$2.99	32 fl. oz.

The Process of Becoming Potential Vendor - Target

Target's process for becoming a cleaning supplies vendor is handled entirely through their website. All buying decisions are also made through their corporate office via www.target.com. Target has a slightly different process for new vendors than Wal-Mart in that they want to make sure your company can meet their demand and other requirements before any buyer sees a product. First, vendors must pass through production and operation hurdles (manufacturing to sustain 1755 stores; a high quality cost competitive product; sufficient product liability insurance; and electronic data interchange capabilities). Once these requirements are met the supplier is evaluated financially by Target. The next step is product submission. Four to six weeks later Target will let the company know if they are interested. Like Wal-Mart, Target managers cannot purchase local products that contain chemicals.

Tier 2 – Regional Retailers

After gaining an understanding of the green cleaning products that discount retail stores like Wal-Mart and Target carry; and obtaining some general knowledge about how they select the vendors and suppliers, the next logical step would be to move down market to what we consider to be the second tier/regional retailers. In doing so, we selected two retailers (grocers' in this case) who placed a high emphasis on selling natural and organic products and as a result, had an existing customer base who placed a value on these products: Whole Foods Market and Wegmans.

Whole Foods Market
Existing "Green" Product Lines – Whole Foods Market

Whole Foods is a natural and organic food market which has over 300 stores in both the United States and the United Kingdom. There are 11 stores in New Jersey which we would consider to be Spruce's target market for beginning stages.

Market research was conducted at the Whole Foods Market in Princeton, New Jersey. This store carried three different brand-name "green"/eco-friendly cleaning products as follows: Clorox Green Works, Nature's Source, and Simple Green. The individual products behind these brand names included cleaning wipes, all-purpose cleaner, glass cleaner, toilet bowl cleaner, bathroom cleaner, and even a concentrated version of an all-purpose cleaner. Below is a summary of Whole Foods cleaning products by brand name, price, and size; as of March 2011:

Clorox Green Works

Cleaning Wipes	$2.99	30 ct.
All-Purpose Cleaner	$2.99	32 fl. oz.
Glass & Surface Cleaner	$2.99	32 fl. oz.
Toilet Bowl Cleaner	$2.79	32 fl. oz.

Simple Green

All Purpose Cleaner (concentrated)	$3.99	32 fl. oz.
All Purpose Cleaner (concentrated)	$7.99	67.6 fl. oz.

Nature's Source

Bathroom Cleaner	$2.99	26 fl. oz.

<u>The Process of Becoming Potential Vendor – Whole Foods Market</u>

Whole Foods Market makes their new vendor selection process (including the steps involved) very clear for potential vendors through a section on their website called "Information for Potential Vendors". Due to the diversity in the customer base amongst their different geographical regions, Whole Foods reviews new products for approval at the regional level. Whole Foods has 10 regional offices within the US. Each regional office has different procedures for reviewing new products and requires that information be submitted in different ways from region to region. Each region has a "coordinator" or "buyer" for different categories of products. Cleaning products would fall into the "grocery" category at Whole Foods, which includes dry goods, dairy, frozen and general categories of products.

We contacted the Mid-Atlantic and Northeast regional offices. Mid-Atlantic consists of stores located in New Jersey (Princeton & Marlton locations), Pennsylvania, Maryland, Ohio, Virginia, Washington D.C., and Kentucky. The Northeast includes stores in Connecticut, New York and New Jersey (excluding Princeton & Marlton). The website provides contact phone numbers for each of these regions. By calling them, we determined the specific people or group that the information should be submitted to. Both regions specifically request that potential product information be submitted via email. The Mid-Atlantic region requests that information be sent directly to an individual (Callie Schmeltz at <u>callie.schmeltz@wholefoods.com</u>), while the Northeast region requests that new product requests be sent to the Grocery Team within this region (<u>negroceryrequest@wholefoods.com</u>).

A detailed email with product information (including images) was submitted to both regions. Unfortunately, the website states that due to the overwhelming volume of new product information submitted, Whole Foods can only respond/contact you if they are interested in the product. After several weeks of no response, we were able to speak with a live person (receptionist) at the Northeast Regional office where she confirmed that typically the group responds within a week to week and a half if there is any interest. Even though there was seemingly no interest in our ReThink Clean product line, we asked if there was someone from the group that we could speak with directly to get some general feedback about our brand, product and overall submission. In a very polite response, she indicated that while the team would like to be able to provide that kind of feedback, they are bombarded with new product emails – which confirmed for us exactly what the website echoed.

Wegmans

Existing "Green" Product Lines - Wegmans

Wegmans is a grocery store that has 77 locations in Massachusetts, Maryland, New Jersey, New York, Pennsylvania and Virginia. In New Jersey there are 7 locations. We believe Wegmans to be a potential retail outlet because it is geared towards a higher end market and they strive to have higher quality products.

Market research was conducted at the Wegmans in Princeton, New Jersey. Wegman's carried 3 different "green" cleaning product brands including: Clorox Green Works, Seventh Generation, and Simple Green. Much like Whole Foods, the individual products behind these brands included, all-purpose cleaner, glass cleaner, toilet bowl cleaner, bathroom cleaner, and even a concentrated version of an all-purpose cleaner. Below is a summary of Wegmans' cleaning products by brand name, price, and size; as of March 2011:

Simple Green

    All Purpose Cleaner (concentrated) $3.99 32 fl. oz.
    All Purpose Cleaner (concentrated) $7.99 67.6 fl. oz.

Seventh Generation

    Glass Cleaner $3.99 32 fl. Oz
    Bathroom Cleaner $3.99 32 fl. Oz
    All Purpose Cleaner (concentrated) $3.99 32 fl. oz.

Clorox Green Works

    All-Purpose Cleaner $2.99 32 fl. oz.
    Toilet Bowl Cleaner $2.99 32 fl. oz.

The Process of Becoming a Potential Vendor - Wegmans

Unlike Whole Foods, Wegmans' new vendor selection process is not made as clear on the website. They seem to provide a lot more information on the website for existing vendors/suppliers, specifically in their 2011 Vendor Guide. Instead of operating somewhat independently under separate regions like Whole Foods, Wegman's operations occur from their Rochester, New York headquarters due to their small reach and only having 77 total stores. We would therefore assume that any Wegmans store would generally carry the same products lines.

There is one form that is referenced in the 2011 Vendor Guide called the "Simplified New Item Set-Up". The website advises to choose the department that fits your product and then complete the new item information that is requested in order for Wegmans to review the introduction of the new item. But we have concluded that this form is only for existing vendors who want to introduce a new product to Wegmans, as it requests some very specific information such as vendor number. As a result, unfortunately, we were not able to get much information as to how to introduce a new product to Wegmans, despite repeated attempts.

Tier 3 – Local/Specialty Retailers

The next tier of retailers we focused on were those that would be considered specialty stores and are owned at a local level. These stores are very into the "green" movement and deem themselves as "natural" stores. This type of store would likely attract customers who are more apt to use or consider using "green" cleaning products. These stores also gave us the most useful information because we were able to have direct access to the people who make the buying decisions. The two stores that we chose to research were Big Bear Natural Foods and Whole Earth Center.

Big Bear Natural Foods

Big Bear Natural Foods has five different locations with three being in New Jersey and two located in Pennsylvania. The New Jersey locations are in Ewing, Lambertville and Pennington while the Pennsylvania locations are in Langhorne and Morrisville. The store carries natural, organic, fresh and whole foods as well as nutritional products, body care products and household goods. The five different stores do not carry all of the same products in terms of brands but do carry the same types of products. The cleaning product selection is very large in terms of the number of brands offered and the types of cleaning these different products do.

Existing "Green" Product Lines – Big Bear

Market research was conducted at the Big Bear in Lambertville, New Jersey. Big Bear carries over a dozen different brands of "green" cleaning products. Seventh Generation is the only brand carried here that we have seen at the other larger retailers as well. Much like the larger retailers, the individual products behind these brands included, all-purpose cleaner, glass cleaner, toilet bowl cleaner, bathroom cleaner, surface, tub & tile, and shower cleaner. There are a few more specialized options compared to the selection we have seen at Tier 1 & Tier 2 retailers. Below is a summary of Big Bear's cleaning products by brand name, price, and size; as of March 2011:

Sun and Earth		
All-Purpose Cleaner	$4.79	22 fl. oz.
Earth Friendly Products		
Surface Cleaner	$3.99	32 fl. oz.
Spring Drop		
Glass Cleaner	$5.99	32 fl. oz.
All-Purpose Cleaner	$7.99	32 fl. oz.
Seventh Generation		
All-Purpose Cleaner	$4.99	32 fl. oz.
Shower Cleaner	$4.99	32 fl. oz.
Tub & Tile Cleaner	$6.19	32 fl. oz.
Glass Cleaner	$6.19	32 fl. oz.

Citrasolv

    All-Purpose Cleaner $4.99 22 fl. oz.

Ecover

    All-Purpose Cleaner $5.69 16.9 fl. oz.
    Glass Cleaner $4.39 16.9 fl. oz.

Earthworm

    All-Purpose Cleaner $6.49 22 fl. oz.
    Bathroom Cleaner $6.49 22 fl. oz.

Naturally It's Clean

    Tube & Tile Cleaner $5.49 16 fl. oz.
    Glass Cleaner $4.99 16 fl. oz.

Biokleen

    All-Purpose Cleaner $5.59 17 fl. oz.
    Bathroom Cleaner $8.99 17 fl. oz.
    Glass Cleaner $5.49 17 fl. oz.

Citraclear

    Glass Cleaner $5.79 32 fl. oz.

Lifetree

    Bathroom Cleaner $5.49 16 fl. oz.

Seaside Naturals

    Glass Cleaner $6.39 16 fl. oz.

Mrs. Meyer's

    All-Purpose Cleaner $8.59 16 fl. oz.
    Shower Cleaner $5.39 16 fl. oz.
    Glass Cleaner $5.39 16 fl. oz.
    Countertop $4.69 16 fl. oz.

The Process of Becoming a Potential Vendor – Big Bear

The president and owner of all five stores is Genya Daukshta who is in charge of determining which new products will be on their shelves. She explained that Big Bear buys mostly from distributors and another employee mentioned the two distributors they typically buy from are Select and Unifi. The Lambertville store is the largest store of the five and sells the most cleaning supplies. Genya told us that there is low interest at the moment for any new cleaning supplies to be carried in their stores. She explained that if they were to carry a new product it would have to be something compelling, have a good price, must be a good product and have an appealing image.

The buying process is straightforward in that Genya would like to see a sample of the product or products with a list of ingredients to determine if the product meets the standards of the store and has a good price point. Once she reviews that information she makes a decision on whether she wants the product in her store or stores. Based on her input, it would be most beneficial to focus on getting the product into the Lambertville store first and possibly spread the product to the other four stores if it has successful sales at the Lambertville location.

Genya is best contacted through email at bigbearnaturalfoods@gmail.com.

Whole Earth Center

Whole Earth Center is a natural and organic grocer that carries local, fresh and "green" products. They carry food products, healthcare products, and home products. There is only one location, which is in Princeton, NJ. The store has two missions which are to provide Princeton with natural and environmentally friendly products while generating money to fund environmental projects and groups.

Existing "Green" Product Lines – Whole Earth Center

Market research was conducted at the Whole Earth Center in Princeton, New Jersey. Whole Earth Center carries seven different brands of "green" cleaning products. Seventh Generation is the only brand carried here that we've seen at other larger retailers. Much like the larger retailers the individual products behind these brands included all-purpose cleaner, glass cleaner, toilet bowl cleaner, bathroom cleaner, surface, tub & tile, and shower cleaner. A few more specialized options compared to the selection we've seen at Tier 1 & Tier 2 retailers yet still a smaller selection then Big Bear. Below is a summary of Whole Earth Center's cleaning products by brand name, price, and size; as of March 2011:

Sun and Earth		
All-Purpose Cleaner	$4.79	22 fl. oz.
Glass Cleaner	$4.79	22 fl. oz.
Earth Friendly Products		
Surface Cleaner	$3.99	32 fl. oz.
Shower Cleaner	$5.39	32 fl. oz.
Toilet Cleaner	$3.99	32 fl. oz.
Seventh Generation		
All-Purpose Cleaner	$4.99	32 fl. oz.
Shower Cleaner	$4.99	32 fl. oz.

Tub & Tile Cleaner	$4.99	32 fl. oz.
Glass Cleaner	$4.99	32 fl. oz.
Bathroom Cleaner	$4.99	32 fl. oz.
Citrasolv		
All-Purpose Cleaner	$4.99	22 fl. oz.
Ecover		
Glass Cleaner	$4.39	16.9 fl. oz.
Biokleen		
All-Purpose Cleaner	$5.59	17 fl. oz.
Glass Cleaner	$5.49	17 fl. oz.
Lifetree		
All-Purpose Cleaner	$6.99	16 fl. oz.
Bathroom Cleaner	$4.49	16 fl. oz.

The Process of Becoming a Potential Vendor – Whole Earth Center

The buying process for Whole Earth Center is fairly straight-forward and simple. The main contact who handles the purchasing is the General Manager, Jennifer Murray. An appointment would be made with her and she would review the information on the product such as ingredients, certifications, story behind it, etc., and look at the sample and make a decision. There is an emphasis on the store having a higher interest in products that are more ecologically friendly and if they are locally produced. Jennifer is available on weekdays and she can be reached at 609-924-7429 to schedule an appointment.

Summary

As private, smaller stores (Tier 3), sales data was not available. Hence, estimates for volume cannot be done. Whereas it is much simpler to get a product into these stores, sales volume also has to be considered, along with the sheer number of green alternatives that are already available. There appears to be a tradeoff in terms of potential market size versus complexity of the new vendor process. Finally, profit margins need to be considered. Pricing is something that would occur much further in the adoption cycle but being competitive will be an issue.

Consumer Website

Overall, we believe the website structure and layout is very professional and user friendly. Therefore, our recommendations for the website will be from a strategic point-of-view with the intention of directing more traffic to the site, and allowing consumers and/or retailers to use it not only for purchasing but also as an educational tool for "green" cleaning products.

Our first recommendation is a strategic one to change the name of the actual website itself. The current name of "Strictly Quarts" could hold a lot of meaning for someone who has experience with liquid, solution, chemical-based products. However, as laypeople, we did not understand the meaning of the website name. Later, as we learned about the business, we can certainly appreciate the idea and thought process behind it but the average consumer does not think of cleaning products in terms of bottle or packaging sizes, and would not understand the creativity behind a name like Strictly Quarts. Therefore, we believe it may be best to change the name to something more "consumer-friendly". Not only could this allow the consumer to associate the name of the website with the products Spruce sells, it could also come up more often when a consumer completes an online search for household cleaning products (search optimization).

Depending on what direction Spruce decides to take based on our recommendations for pursuing the consumer market with the ReThink Clean product line, our suggestions for the website name vary. If the pursuit of ReThink Clean happens, then we believe that the site should be focused on that product line and be named something similar to ReThink Clean or simply the name of the product itself, depending on the availability of names. This will not only stand out as a marketing tool but also can be used to show potential retailers to help sell the product to them. If the ReThink Clean product line is not pursued, then we recommend a name that is generalized and relates to cleaning; or contains the word "clean" or "cleaning." We believe that it will let the consumer understand what the website is actually offering when the name is presented.

Our second recommendation is related to the layout of the website and the location of the "Log-In" for returning customers. The log in for customers who have established an account at the website should be moved to the top right corner either above or below the search bar. This location would be easier for returning customers, which will in turn make them more satisfied when visiting the site and purchasing products. At the moment, the site's homepage is too long vertically and the log in is located at the very bottom of the page, which is not apparent upon a quick visit to the site. This recommendation would not only assist in the purchasing process for returning customers, it will also make the bottom of the page more aesthetically pleasing.

A third recommendation relates to the content of the website. We recommend adding an educational aspect to the website allowing the consumer to gain knowledge and awareness of why "green" cleaning products should be chosen and used over regular cleaning products. If the ReThink Clean line is pursued then this content should be related to that product line and its capabilities in addition to what makes the produce "green." This information would be more compelling to the consumer if the website provided simple, fact-based bullet points on the benefits of using eco-friendly cleaning products. As an example, next to the all-purpose cleaner it might read: 'By using this eco-friendly product over a traditional one, you are saving 2 trees', or 'By using this glass cleaner over its traditional counterpart, you save a family of hawks since the production process does not harm the environment' etc.. This would allow consumers to relate the use of these products to everyday life and give them a better understanding of why they should choose "green" cleaning products over regular cleaning products. If the ReThink Clean product line is not pursued than we recommend having the education section generalized on "green" cleaning products without a focus on any specific products.

The fourth and fifth recommendations involve the pages bar at the top of the website in which the consumer would use to navigate to different features of the site itself. The first of these recommendations is that we feel the "MSDS search" is somewhat unnecessary from a consumer standpoint. Our team, when viewing the site as a consumer, did not know what this feature was and had to look up the meaning of MSDS. For this reason, we believe that it does not need to be such a prominent feature on the site, if a feature at all. It seems that it is something that would be more important to the industrial purchasers than to the consumer market. The feature can still be on the site in case a consumer is interested in the MSDS information; however, we believe it should be placed at the bottom or somewhere that will not cause confusion for a regular consumer. Another feature on the pages bar we recommend should be changed is the "resources" feature. We believe that the pages which are listed under this feature should be their own features in the pages bar. "Resources" should just be replaced by the four other pages which are currently under the feature. These features will allow for more information to be given to the consumers because they will understand those terms more than they would understand what "resources" would include.

Our final recommendation involves the color scheme for the website and we believe that it should be softer and less industrial looking. The black is too industrial-looking and the site should be brighter so it is more attractive to the consumer. Also, brighter colors will associate better with "green" products and will correspond better with the colors of the products featured on the website.

VII. Conclusion & Final Recommendations

The goal of the project was to provide recommendations to Spruce Industries on an effective approach to enter the consumer market. Spruce currently conducts almost 100% of its business in the commercial marketplace and has an interest in increasing sales and profits by selling their products in the consumer market. Spruce has made some initial progress towards this goal through the development of a website focused on the consumer market, which would allow individuals to make online purchases of household-sized cleaning products. While the use of a professionally designed website is one avenue towards gaining a marginal share of the consumer cleaning product market, as a team we felt that the large majority of consumers purchase these products from brick and mortar retailers. As a result, we decided to consider the possibility of accessing this market by considering the feasibility of obtaining retail shelf space for specific Spruce products. Below are our recommendations based on the research that was performed and analyzed as described in the preceding sections of this report.

The market for "green" cleaning products and "green" products in general is growing and will eventually become the standard in the cleaning industry. We believe now is an appropriate time to enter the green-cleaning consumer product market before it becomes overly saturated with competitors and the barriers of entry become even greater. The largest challenge facing the growth of green cleaning products relates to consumer behavior; getting people to change habits of buying traditional cleaning products to purchasing green cleaning products. An important factor in altering or changing existing consumer behavior involves educating consumers on the benefits of using eco-friendly cleaning products. Not only can the website be employed as a purchasing agent, it can also be used in the process of educating the general public about the benefits and trends toward green cleaning.

Aside from the website recommendations that are described in detail in the prior section, we have two additional recommendations for Spruce Industries as it relates to their potential further pursuit of the consumer cleaning product market. Both of these recommendations are directly related to the utilization of the ReThink Clean brand and product line. To recap, we obtained detailed information from selected stores that fall into three separate levels of retailers based on size and scope. The purpose of obtaining this information has allowed us to evaluate the potential feasibility and opportunity associated with obtaining retail shelf space as a means to access the consumer market. If Spruce decides to take any action at all towards consumers at the retail level, we recommend that it target only what we have defined as Tier 3 retailers on a trial basis (Local/Specialty stores). Our second recommendation involves the task of locating a new retailer tier that is larger than a Tier 3 but smaller than our Tier 2 (large regional).

We do not recommend Tier 1 (national) or Tier 2 (regional) retailers for many of the same reasons. While national retailers such as Wal-Mart or Target carry a limited number of "green" cleaning products, the barriers towards becoming a potential vendor are extremely high (especially for smaller vendors like Spruce). Spruce does not have the resources to supply enough product for all of Wal-Mart's 4,300 stores and Target's 1,755 stores. Also, due to the stringent submission process for products containing chemicals (explained in the "Process & Feasibility of Obtaining Retail Shelf-Space" section of this report), it would not be possible to manufacture and supply enough of the product for possible retail distribution. It was important, however, to gain an understanding of the national retail environment as it relates to green cleaning process and accessibility of new vendors. While the Tier 2 (regional) stores may seem more accessible from a potential vendor viewpoint, we found the barriers to entry for these retailers to still be extremely difficult. Wegmans performs its vendor selection process from its Rochester, NY headquarters, and requires those vendors to supply the product to all 70+ retail locations. While supporting this amount of manufacturing and supply would likely be attainable for the Spruce/Misco relationship, gaining access to the 'new-vendor selection group' within Wegmans proved to be more difficult than expected. Whole Foods new vendor selection process on the other hand, occurs at the local level, which we believed would make it easier to access this group within one or two of their regions. Given the lack of response after contacting these groups with ReThink Clean product information, this may be a testament to the high volume of inquiries that they receive by email on a daily/weekly basis. While we were unable to obtain feedback from either of the Tier 2 regional retailers, Spruce could always pursue it further. At this point however, given the amount of information we received within the timing of this consulting project, we would not recommend that initial penetration into the consumer market be through the Tier 2 regional retailers.

While the Tier 3 (local/specialized) retailers had a small number of stores, we found that the competition within the "green" cleaning product category among these retailers to be the highest of all. Consistent with the high level of saturation of competition, the barriers to entry are also extremely low. An advantage to low barriers is the access a vendor gets to managers and owners of these stores, as these contacts typically make all of the vendor decisions themselves. While the necessary profit margin levels are likely to be achieved when selling the ReThink Clean product line through local retailers, the expected sales volume levels would be low. If Spruce is interested in taking small steps towards pursuing the consumer market at the retail store level, we would recommend doing so through what we have deemed as a Tier 3 (local/specialized) retailer for a 6-12 month trial period. While the financial incentive in doing so may not present itself initially, there is not much of an initial investment, and the downside risk is minimal to a 6-12 month trial period. It would also allow Spruce to gauge the consumer reaction towards the ReThink Clean brand and product line. If the reaction is positive and Spruce wanted to introduce this product to other small retailers, it would be easier to do so.

Separate from the local retailer trial period, we would recommend developing/locating a fourth tier of retailers to consider piloting the ReThink Clean brand. After we analyzed the research we had gathered on the three different tiers of retailers, we observed that there was a significant difference in size between Tier 2 and Tier 3 retailers (regional and local). The smallest of the regional retailers we selected (Wegmans) had approximately 70 stores, which made it difficult to gain access to those who make the decisions about new vendors. The largest of the local retailers only had 4-5 store locations. Therefore, our idea of a fourth tier would be a larger local or smaller regional retailer that may have 10-25 stores where the managers/owners would still be accessible and the potential sales volume would exist to make any further investment in the consumer market worth the time. This type of retailer could be engaged either during a 6-12 month trial period with a small local retailer or after Spruce has had the chance to evaluate the results of that trial period.

We have done additional research to give Spruce some examples of stores that may fit these criteria. The examples we have come up with are Foodtown and Shop N Bag. Foodtown has locations in New York, New Jersey and Pennsylvania with 28 locations in New Jersey. Shop N Bag has locations in New Jersey and Pennsylvania with 29 stores in total. We believe these examples for a possible Tier 4 of stores may be more lucrative and promising for expansion in the consumer market for the ReThink Clean brand.

VIII.   Appendices

A) Consumer Survey

This survey is being conducted for a consulting project by a group of students from Rider University in regards to the consumer's perception of "green" or eco-friendly products.
1.) Do you currently purchase and use "Green" or Eco-friendly cleaning products?

○ Yes

○ No

○ Not sure

2.) What type of cleaner do you use the most? Rank the following in order of most used to least used. 1 being most and 5 being least.

Degreaser	
Glass Cleaner	
All Surface Cleaner	
Bathroom Cleaner	
Other	

3.) When purchasing cleaning products what factors influence your decision? Please rank the following criteria from most influential to least influential. 1 being most and 5 being least.

Price	
Brand	
Green or Eco-friendly	
Look of product	
Other	

4.) Out of the following 3 logos, which have you heard of?

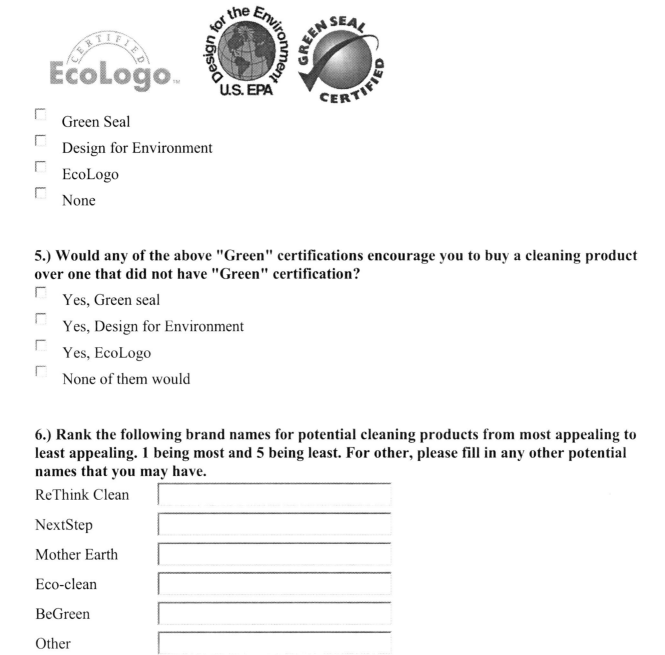

☐ Green Seal

☐ Design for Environment

☐ EcoLogo

☐ None

5.) Would any of the above "Green" certifications encourage you to buy a cleaning product over one that did not have "Green" certification?

☐ Yes, Green seal

☐ Yes, Design for Environment

☐ Yes, EcoLogo

☐ None of them would

6.) Rank the following brand names for potential cleaning products from most appealing to least appealing. 1 being most and 5 being least. For other, please fill in any other potential names that you may have.

ReThink Clean	
NextStep	
Mother Earth	
Eco-clean	
BeGreen	
Other	

B) References

About Us. (2011). Retrieved April 21, 2011, from
   http://www.thriftwayshopnbag.com/AboutUs.aspx

Big Bear Natual Foods. (2010). Retrieved from http://www.bigbearnaturalfoods.com

Case, Scot. "A Clean Sweep." *GovPro*. Penton Publishing, Oct. 2004. Web. 23 Jan. 2011.
   <http://www.govpro.com>.

EcoLogo. (2011). Retrieved from http://www.environmentalchoice.com/en/

Fleenor, Gail D. "A Greener Clean." *Progressive Grocer* July 2010: 66-68. *Business Source
   Premier*. Web. 23 Jan. 2011.

Garrison, Kelsey. "Green and Clean?" *Fitness Business Pro* Jan. 2009: 50-55. *Business Source
   Premier*. Web. 23 Jan. 2011.

Greenseal. (2011). Retrieved from http://www.greenseal.org

"How to Partner, Get the DfE Label on a Product." *EPA*. N.p., 31 Jan. 2011. Web. 4 Feb. 2011.
   <http://www.epa.gov/dfe/pubs/projects/formulat/about.htm>.

Neff, Jack. "Growth Market as progressive schools push green agenda." *Advertising Age* 6 Sept.
   2010: 20-22. *Business Source Premier*. Web. 23 Jan. 2011.

Store Locations. (2011). Retrieved April 21, 2011, from   http://foodtown.mywebgrocer.com/
   StoreLocator.aspx?s=141844488&g=a02ba739-fe5d-4053-ae01-
   65a707db6707&uc=51AB135

Target. (2011). Retrieved from http://www.target.com

Walmart. (2011). Retrieved from http://www.walmart.com

Wegmans. (n.d.). Retrieved from http://www.wegmans.com

Whole Earth Center. (2011). Retrieved from http://www.wholeearthcenter.com

Whole Foods Market. (2011). Retrieved from http://www.wholefoodsmarket.com

Williamson, Julie E. "Green cleaning gaining ground." *Healthcare Purchasing News* 33.4 (Apr.
   2009): 32-36. *Business Source Premier*. Web. 23 Jan. 2011.

C) Engagement Letter- See earlier sample in Appendix 3A

Appendix 3B: Sample Consulting Report

Community Food Bank of NJ "Grains for Good" Final Report

December 2007

(This report is included to enhance the learning experience for the student. It shows an excellent example of a consulting project. The client has given permission for it to be used and sections/information may be disguised).

Executive Summary   102

1. Introduction   103

2. Marketing Analysis   103

3. Operations Analysis   109

4. Financial Model   114

5. Conclusions and Recommendations   116

Executive Summary

Of the four product options considered for the "Grains for Good" brand, bagel chips present the best chance for success. Based on primary and secondary research they scored significantly higher than the other products with respect to consumer's expectations, their likelihood to purchase and the price they would be willing to pay. Bagel chip production at the projected volume level fits within the constraints on space and capital of the Community Food Bank of New Jersey's (CFBNJ).

The "Grains for Good" brand and product concept are well suited for a cause related marketing campaign and align well with CFBNJ's programs. The message that "100% of profits benefit the Community FoodBank of New Jersey" is very attractive to survey participants. Likewise, the survey revealed high CFBNJ brand awareness and concern about hunger issues among respondents. Packaging containing effective message is critical to influencing consumer purchasing decisions.

Primary and secondary research indicates that the quality of the product, in this case taste and consistency, is crucial to a successful cause-related marketing campaign. The recipe for the product must be appealing to the customers and the packaging and promotional materials must convey the "100% Proceeds" message to enable CFBNJ to charge a premium price for the item. Customers are willing to pay up to a 20% price premium for the product.

The "Grains for Good" product requires a strong commitment from the retail bakery-cafe company, which is its supplier of bread donations. This company must supply adequate bread donations that can be efficiently used as the raw material for production. It must be able to process sales and ensure 100% of the proceeds are transferred to CFBNJ in a timely manner. Furthermore, this retail bakery-cafe company must be willing to facilitate additional primary research to determine how receptive its customers are to various recipes, packaging options and message communication. Additionally, it must provide promotional support in the form of in-store merchandising space and space for items like window posters, table tents, and brochures. The integrated involvement of this leading retail bakery-cafe company is critical to the success of "Grains for Good."

Financial modeling shows input variables have the potential for wide variability, making the prediction of this project's success uncertain. Two key variables include the cost of labor and the quantity of sales. A "break-even" scenario requires selling 12 items in each of the retail bakery-cafe company's 42 stores per week and at zero labor costs, a significant hurdle for project success.

Overall, the expected income from "Grains for Good" may not be significant enough to justify the time, money and effort required to execute the project within the parameters explored by this analysis. CFBNJ must carefully review the analysis and recommendations presented herein to determine if the project warrants further exploration or if CFBNJ's limited resources are more profitably deployed elsewhere. Should CFBNJ choose to proceed, next steps include creating a bagel chip recipe and validating it through tastings among potential customers Furthermore, engaging the retail bakery-cafe company to discuss and confirm its willingness to partner with CFBNJ to collect additional primary research, supply adequate usable bread products, provide in-store promotional, merchandising and logistics support is critical.

1. Introduction

The Community Food Bank of New Jersey (CFBNJ) has retained the services of the Rutgers Business School MBA Interfunctional Consulting Program to evaluate the feasibility of a for-profit venture utilizing donated raw materials received from a leading retail bakery-cafe company to create a bread-based product for sale in its company stores. The product would utilize the "Grains for Good" brand as developed by CFBNJ. The venture is designed to provide income to support CFBNJ's non-profit operations and potentially provide employment to community members.

2. Marketing Analysis
A. Market Size

In order to project possible sales and market share for a CFBNJ product, the team conducted extensive research to understand the current market size, growth and household penetration for four products: breadcrumbs, croutons, bread pudding, and bagel chips. Our research yielded data for breadcrumbs and croutons, showing breadcrumbs with the largest market share followed by croutons. Data on bread pudding was negligible indicating this may be a novel idea for the U.S. marketplace. Bagel chip data was also scarce; however, a significant volume of chips are sold fresh through small local bagel shops rather than packaged through retailers. This data comes from supermarkets and therefore one must be cautious that supermarket data is not representative of the retail bakery-cafe company's customers.

B. Consumer Trends

When looking at the general trends of the snack food market, the healthy snacks segment has seen an increase of 6% in 2006. Over 60% of healthy snack eaters are looking for a healthier alternative. Recent health concerns among U.S. residents show better-for-you snacks have become the biggest trend in the salty snack category. Whole grain, multi-grain and baked snacks are increasing in popularity. In keeping with the trend, baked bagel chips that are multi-grain or whole grain are likely to be viewed as healthy. Consumer packaged goods companies are introducing new lines of baked chips as well as new lines of multi-grain snack products in order to revive their brands. Companies are introducing products flavored with fruit, vegetable, and tomato basil in an effort to boost sales.

As the product claims increase, so does the confusion to their true meanings. The biggest confusion in product claims is the difference between whole grain and multi-grain. Whole grains are seeds of various plants that have all three main parts: bran, endosperm, and germ. Neither the FDA nor the USDA has established final regulations on whole grain labeling. However, some limitations on whole grain health claims, as well as certain standards of identification have been set by the FDA.

C. Cause Related Marketing

Most non-profit ventures into the for-profit space are known as cause related marketing (CRM). CRM is defined as when companies partner with charitable organizations, generate revenue through the sale of products and return a portion of the revenue back to the cause. There are three major categories of CRM: green marketing, breast cancer charities, and then all others. CRM campaigns have seen rapid growth since 2001 and they are estimated to be worth three times the marketing expenditure. Consumers are willing to pay 5% more on average to support a good cause.

Several large corporations are known for their support of charities through CRM. Ben & Jerry's, Newman's Own, and Burt's Bees are recognized leaders in this space. Characteristics of CRM market leaders include: consonance of values/ mission between corporation and non-profit, integration, transparency and long-term support   It is imperative that these qualities are present in licensing and CRM agreements to safeguard monetary support and company reputation.

Based on CRM research, the relationship between CFBNJ and the leading retail bakery-cafe company exhibits desirable leader characteristics. Additionally, the relationship between this company and America's Second Harvest demonstrates a commitment to social causes

The largest driver of awareness for CRM is product packaging, followed by advertising. Product packaging must be compelling enough to draw the customer in and encourage purchase. CRM alone will not make a bad product more appealing but it does make a difference. Females and households with children demonstrate a positive affinity towards these campaigns. Research shows that there is an opportunity to charge a small price premium with these campaigns.

An analysis of the types of products that can be used in cause related marketing show food and beverage items are the clear winners. Among the list of causes that consumers would like to see supported include education, child welfare, poverty, and local concerns. The CFBNJ venture with the leading retail bakery-cafe company reflects both the causes consumers would like to support and the products they would expect to support them.

Key takeaways from the CRM research:

- CRM between CFBNJ and the Leading Retail Bakery-Cafe Company is promising. The relationship exhibits leader characteristics that are critical to success.

- CFBNJ must select a product that is intrinsically desirable to consumers. Consumers will not buy products they do not use or need simply due to a CRM campaign.

- Although consumers are willing to pay a premium on products that support a cause, the price premium can not be excessive.

- Women and families with children are more likely to respond to CRM.

D. Competitive Products

The four products considered varied greatly in their product range and features.

The bread crumb category contains the most number of competitor products, with Progresso as the leading brand. The cost for bread crumbs ranged widely, from $0.13 to $1.33 per ounce, with the 8 ounces as the most common packaging size. The cost variation is directly correlated to the health or other claims of the product, as demonstrated by the highest priced product, gluten free Amaranth crumbs. The most popular packaging for bread crumbs is a fiberboard or cardboard canister.

There are limited number of product offerings and brands in the crouton category. The cost for bread croutons ranges from $0.36 to $0.80 per ounce, with 5 ounces as the most common packaging size. The most common packaging for croutons was a free-standing pouch style bag.

The bread pudding mix category is small with only a few products available, predominantly from specialty manufacturers. Prices range from $0.28 to $0.42 per ounce, and packaging and volume varied. None of the products include bread or bread products as part of the mix.

There are limited product offerings in the bagel chip category, mainly due to unbranded bagel chips produced in local bakeries. The cost for bagel chips ranges from $0.45 to $1.75 per ounce, with 6 ounces as the most common size. The highest priced item (Banana Moon) is packaged as a specialty souvenir item. Most pre-packaged bagel chips are not made from "real" bagels and are offered in a variety of flavors.

Key takeaways from the competitive product research and analysis:

- Bread Crumb prices range from $1.39 to $4.49. The greater the claims of the product – organic, gluten free, wheat free – the higher the price of the product.

- Bread Crouton prices range from $1.79 to $3.99. There is no obvious correlation between product claims/features and prices.

- Bread Pudding is a specialized product with few pre-packaged products available. All products are powder mixes that require the addition of other ingredients, including bread. Prices range from $4.95 to $6.75.

- Bagel Chip prices range from $2.69 to $2.99 with few pre-packaged varieties available.

E. Primary Research: Objectives

The objectives of the primary research effort were

1. To develop market-based recommendations for the product, packaging, and pricing decisions.

2. To test the relative impact of messaging options which convey the cause marketing benefit and the healthy product benefit.

3. To measure consumer awareness of CFBNJ and hunger issues in general.

4. To better understand the shopping behavior of the retail bakery-cafe company's consumers and ascertain whether packaged food products can be successful in this channel.

F. Primary Research: Methodology

The methodology chosen was a quantitative, online survey which included question sets that explored each of the objectives listed above. The survey was structured so as to isolate certain consumer preferences. For example, the questions around product and price preferences were placed in the beginning of the survey to capture a "baseline" measure of those preferences before the idea of cause marketing was introduced. Later, questions specific to the proposed cause marketing efforts enabled measurement of cause marketing's incremental effect.

G. Primary Research: Sample Characteristics

The consumer sample surveyed consisted of 153 individuals who had dined or shopped in the leading retail bakery-cafe company stores in the prior year. The survey was fielded to the Rutgers community via email between 11/16/2007 and 11/23/2007. It was constructed using and hosted by SurveyMonkey.com.

Key aspects of the sample characteristics are as follows:

- Age Group: All age groups were represented, except for "Under 18." The largest single age group, with 34% of the sample, was "26-35."
- Gender: The majority of the respondents (66%) were female.
- Occupation: The vast majority of respondents (77%) were employed full-time.
- Education: An unusually high percentage of respondents (55%) listed their highest level of education as "Graduate Degree." This is not surprising because the survey was fielded among the Rutgers University community.
- Number of Children: Most respondents (62%) had no children.
- Marital status: 60% of those surveyed were married.

H. Primary Research: Results

Many of the findings are summarized as a "top 2 box" percentage. This means that the particular question had a 5-point response scale (e.g. very likely to purchase, somewhat likely to purchase, may or may not purchase, somewhat unlikely to purchase, not at all likely to purchase). The top 2 box score is the percentage of respondents who selected one of the top two responses. For example, using the response scale above, the top 2 box score would be the percentage of respondents who selected "very likely to purchase" or "somewhat likely to purchase." This top 2 box percentage is used to measure how many respondents are likely to purchase the particular product. The top 2 box method is a widely accepted way of summarizing market research data.

Throughout the survey the retail bakery-cafe company that is partnering with CFBNJ is not exclusively mentioned. Instead, the questions refer in general to "bakery café restaurants (such as Panera, Au Bon Pain, or Atlanta Bread Company)". This approach was chosen because it prevented the survey from revealing the specifics of this business idea and it enabled the team to field the survey rapidly without necessitating approvals from specific companies.

The survey explored 3 different product concepts: breadcrumbs, croutons, and bagel chips. When consumers were asked how likely they were to purchase one of these packaged food items when visiting a bakery café restaurant, they revealed a low likelihood to purchase, particularly for the breadcrumb and crouton products. 14% of respondents were likely to purchase croutons, and only 9% were likely to purchase breadcrumbs. 28% of respondents were likely to purchase bagel chips. Although this was not an overwhelmingly positive response, it is twice the likelihood of purchase as the next-best product concept, croutons.

The survey revealed that consumers prefer seasoned "Italian style" breadcrumbs over unseasoned breadcrumbs by a 3 to 1 margin. Consumers were more evenly split around the issue of breadcrumb texture. When asked whether they would prefer traditional fine breadcrumbs, coarse panko-style breadcrumbs, or both textures sold together in a combination package, 39% chose fine breadcrumbs, 35% chose panko-style, and 26% chose both.

Across all 3 product ideas, the survey revealed that resealable bags were strongly preferred over the other packaging ideas: a "Rustic paper bag with window," a "Rustic paper bag without window," and a "Printed box." For each product idea, between 60% and 70% of respondents indicated that they prefer the resealable bag. A significant minority of respondents indicated that packaging would be an important part of their purchase decision: between 30% and 40% across all products.

When testing health-related product claims, the survey demonstrated that consumers recognize little distinction between the "whole grain" and "multi-grain" claims; 82% of respondents would be more likely to purchase a product with a "whole grain" claim versus 80% for a "multi-grain" claim. This is a significant finding for this project, because "whole grain" has a specific definition which cannot be achieved based on the raw materials available from the Retail Bakery-Cafe Company stores. There is a much better chance of developing a product that can deliver on a multi-grain claim.

The price expectation questions revealed that most consumers expect to pay under $3.00 for one of these products: 54% of respondents expected an 8 oz. package of breadcrumbs to cost between $2.00 and $2.99; 63% of respondents expected a 5 oz. package of croutons to cost between $2.00 and $2.99. For a 6 oz. package of bagel chips, price expectations were more evenly split between the $2.00-$2.99 range (46%) and the $3.00-$3.99 range (44%). Across all three products, only a small percentage of respondents expected to pay over $4.00. Once these baseline price expectations were established, respondents were asked how much more they would be willing to spend for a packaged food product where 100% of the profits benefit CFBNJ. The median percentage premium that consumers would be willing to pay was 20%.

The survey showed that most consumers – 53% – expected to find bagel chips for sale at a bakery café restaurant, but that a low percentage of consumers expected to find breadcrumbs or croutons, 12% and 26%, respectively.

As described in the objectives above, this survey was also intended to explore consumer awareness of CFBNJ and hunger issues generally. The survey indicated that 87% of respondents are concerned about fighting hunger in local communities. 82% of respondents have heard of CFBNJ. A somewhat lower percentage of respondents – 59% – indicated that they were familiar with the charitable work that CFBNJ does to fight hunger and poverty.

Respondents were exposed to four different cause marketing message variants and asked how much more likely they would be to purchase a product because of each: "Grains for Good" 100% of profits benefit The Community Food Bank of New Jersey, "Grains for Good" supporting The Community Food Bank of New Jersey, "Grains for Good fighting hunger and poverty in our community" and "Support The Community Food Bank of New Jersey in its fight against hunger and poverty." The strongest message, by a significant margin, was "'Grains for Good' 100% of profits benefit The Community Food Bank of New Jersey." 86% of respondents indicated that they would be more likely to purchase a given product based on this message.

A series of questions were used to develop a better understanding of the shopping behavior by customers of the retail bakery café company, and the opportunity that exists for selling packaged food items through this channel. The survey results show that 56% of respondents visited bakery café restaurants at least monthly. 78% of respondents visit bakery café restaurants to eat a meal or snack rather than to shop the bakery. Most respondents – 54% – have actually browsed packaged food items in a bakery café restaurant, and 32% have actually bought a packaged food item. This suggests that the bakery-cafe company distribution channel is at least somewhat compatible with packaged food items.

As bagel chips appear to the be the most promising product idea from a consumer perspective, a bivariate analysis was conducted to segment out respondents who were "somewhat likely" or "very likely" to buy bagel chips and see whether their responses to the survey questions vary significantly from the overall sample. For the most part, these consumers' responses were very similar to the overall survey results. A few interesting differences did emerge:

- 61% of the respondents who were likely to buy bagel chips indicated that packaging was important to their purchase decision, versus 38% among the entire sample.

- 7% of the respondents who were likely to buy bagel chips visit bakery café restaurants to shop the bakery, versus only 3% among the overall sample.

- 30% of the respondents who were likely to buy bagel chips visit bakery café restaurants to both shop the bakery and eat a meal or snack, versus 19% among the entire sample.

These distinctions illustrate that packaging will be very important to the success of a bagel chip product. They also yield a merchandising insight – that bagel chip buyers are more likely than the average consumer to browse the bakery counter at the retail bakery-cafe company. This could be helpful information when determining where these products should be displayed in-store.

I. Primary Research: Recommendations

The following are recommendations based on the information and insights gathered in the primary research:

1. Proceed with the operations and financial analysis of the bagel chip concept. The survey indicated that the bagel chip product concept has the best chance for market success as compared to breadcrumbs and croutons. It is also congruent with the Retail Bakery-Cafe Company partner of CFBNJ, in the mind of the consumer, whereas most consumers would not expect to find breadcrumbs or croutons for sale at their stores.

2. Package the bagel chips in resealable bags. The resealable bag packaging concept was far more desirable than any of the other options under consideration. This makes sense, as resealable bags have functional value that the other packaging ideas lack.

3. Price the bagel chips at $3.99. The price expectation data showed that few customers would be willing to pay more than $4.00. Respondents were almost evenly split between an expectation that bagel chips should cost $2.00-$2.99 and $3.00-$3.99. Factoring in the 20% premium consumers would be willing to pay if 100% of proceeds benefit CFBNJ, $3.99 is an appropriate price.

4. Utilize a "multi-grain" claim if the final product composition supports it. This will enable the product to capitalize on the trend toward healthy, whole wheat and whole grain snacks. Consumers recognize little distinction between "multi-grain" and "whole grain."

5. Utilize this claim to promote the cause marketing aspect of the product: "100% of profits benefit The Community Food Bank of New Jersey." The survey demonstrated that this claim was significantly more influential than the others tested, and it highlights the unique value of this particular cause marketing arrangement between CFBNJ and the Leading Retail Bakery-

Cafe Company. Also, the 20% price premium that consumers would be willing to pay for a product that supports CFBNJ was based on informing respondents that 100% of the profits would go to the Food Bank.

6. Within the "Grains for Good" promotional materials (posters, flyers, tent cards, etc.) communicate CFBNJ's specific efforts to fight hunger and poverty. The survey demonstrated CFBNJ's tremendous brand awareness in the state, but indicated that consumers were less familiar with their particular programs. One hypothesis is that the ubiquitous "Check Out Hunger" program is responsible for building such strong brand awareness.

7. When making merchandising decisions (such as where to position the products in-store), note that most of the Retail Bakery-Cafe Company customers will be visiting for a meal or snack, but that bagel chip buyers are more likely than the average customer to visit the bakery counter.

3. Operations Analysis

A. Labeling Requirements

All food product labels must conform to government regulations. As of January 1, 2006 the FDA requires all producers to follow two rules: plain English language wording and no hidden allergens on food labels. This new regulation defines major food allergens as any of the following:

- The "Big 8" food allergens: milk, egg, fish (e.g., bass, flounder), crustacean shellfish (e.g., crab, lobster or shrimp), tree nuts (e.g., almonds, pecans or walnuts), wheat, peanuts and soybeans.

- A food ingredient that contains protein derived from a food in the "Big 8" category, except any highly refined oil derived from the "Big 8" or any ingredient derived from such highly refined oil.

There are two options for meeting the labeling requirements for food allergens. One, use a content statement which means that the word "contains" is followed by a list of all the major food allergens contained in the product. This phrase must be immediately adjacent to the ingredient statement. Two, use a parenthetical listing, which means that intertwined within the list of ingredients, the plain English name of all food allergens is included in parentheses behind their common or usual names; e.g. casein (milk).

On February 16, 2006 the FDA established that whole-grain foods should contain the three key ingredients of cereal grains: bran (the fiber-filled outer part of the kernel), endosperm (the inner part and usually all that is left in most processed grains) and the germ (the heart of the grain kernel). Additionally, the FDA recommends that these three ingredients need to be present in the same relative proportion as they exist naturally -- a way to be sure that manufacturers do not add back small amounts of each ingredient to highly processed food and then call it whole grain. The new definition is only a recommendation and is not yet legally enforceable.

In order for CFBNJ to claim their product as whole grain, it is important to know what ingredients are used to produce each product and in what proportions.

A preliminary exploration of preservatives used in bakery products showed that propionates are used extensively as a preservative in bakery products. They are effective against molds and bacterial spores and have no known side-effects. Options include propionic acid, sodium propionate, calcium propionate, and potassium propionate and whey powder. All of these antimicrobials are related to propionic acid, which occurs naturally in strawberries, apples, violet leaves, grains, and cheese.

B. Logistics

CFBNJ has a full function kitchen onsite operating for the purpose of training students and providing food service programs. Inside the kitchen, the major equipment includes a walk-in size Hobart commercial oven with carrousel (Model HSG 400 Gas Burner) and a Hobart mixer with grate attachment (Model H340). Currently, CFBNJ picks up bread from the Retail Bakery-Cafe Company three times a week with an N-series Isuzu 16-foot refrigerated truck. Additionally CFBNJ also visits several other Retail Bakery-Cafe Company locations. In the future, CFBNJ plans to pickup bread from more locations.

The major raw materials of this production plan come from retail bakery-cafe company locations in the New Jersey area. CFBNJ is currently in charge of the day old bread pickup from these locations. Therefore, the project team suggests CFBNJ utilize the same truck to ship out our finished products to the retail stores for display. There are 10 bakery-cafe company locations within 13 miles of CFBNJ's Hillside location. There are another 32 locations in New Jersey beyond this radius. In order to achieve higher transportation efficiency, the project team suggests CFBNJ coordinate with the Retail Bakery-Cafe Company to determine the best routing and scheduling. This company utilizes a visual routing and scheduling software, InterGIS, to manage the transportation and logistics among its stores.

C. Production Flow

The project team summarized the expected production flow based on recipes provided and online research.

Bagel Chips
Step 1: Slicing the bagels.
Step 2: Seasoning for either savory or sweet flavor (optional).
Step 3: Baking in the oven for about an hour at 375°F.
Step 4: Packaging and labeling after cooling.
Note: The bottleneck in this production flow is expected to be the slicing process.

Bread Crumbs
Step 1: Slicing the bread.
Step 2: Baking in the oven for about an hour at 375°F.
Step 3: Finely grinding the dried slices.
Step 4: Packaging and labeling after cooling.
Note: The bottleneck in this production flow is expected to be the grinding process.

Croutons
Step 1: Slicing the bread.
Step 2: Cubing the slices.
Step 3: Seasoning for savory flavor (butter, oil, spices, salt).
Step 4: Baking in the oven for about an hour at 375°F.
Step 5: Packaging and labeling after cooing.
Note: The bottleneck in this production flow is expected to be the seasoning process.

Bread Pudding Mix
Step 1: Slicing the bread.
Step 2: Cubing the slices.
Step 3: Baking in the oven for about an hour at 375°F.
Step 4: Adding dry mix of egg/milk/flavor powders.
Step 5: Packaging and labeling after cooing.
Note: The bottleneck in this production flow is expected to be the baking process.

D. Raw Materials

The Retail Bakery-Cafe Company that is partnering with CFBNJ produces a large selection of bagels and breads in its bakery. In the bagel selection there are two major categories, sweet and savory. The sweet items include cinnamon crunch, Dutch apple and raisin, blueberry, cranberry walnut, gingerbread, and French toast. The savory items include Asiago cheese, everything, plain, whole grain, and sesame. In the bread selection, there are two major categories, artisan and specialty, which include 33 varieties in total. Raw material inflows to CFBNJ will be highly variable based upon the overproduction in each Retail Bakery-Cafe Company store – this creates a significant challenge for the project. The finished product will require a tasty recipe that can work around input constraints as well as consumer tastes. Additionally, labeling requirements will change based on the inputs.

E. Machinery

For bagel chip production, CFBNJ may be able to utilize its on hand deli slicer to slice bagels. This will minimize initial capital investment. If later production scale up is considered, an industrial type bagel slicer should be acquired. The Hobart walk-in commercial oven with carrousel can be utilized for drying. Other machines CFBNJ may consider for later scale-up include: seasoning tools, packaging tools, a bag sealing machine, and an auto-filling machine.

In every operation cost and efficiency are always tradeoffs. CFBNJ must make a decision on the volume and speed of production. We have provided many options for each type of operation and desired production volume.

Bagel Slicer

The texture of bagels is thicker than regular breads. It is not an option to slice the bagel with a bread knife as this will not achieve consistent thickness; bagel slicing must be done with a machine. One option is the deli slicer already owned by CFBNJ. The second option is a bagel slicer which can be built for slicing either horizontally or vertically. Bagel slicing machines which are suitable for bagel chip creation are not standard stock items; machines are customized to order based upon user specifications.

Bread Slicer

Two solutions for bread slicing are available in the marketplace: a countertop slicing machine and a commercial slicing machine. They both can create the desired product outcomes but manpower and handling times will vary between machines.

Cubing Machine

For croutons, the cubing machine can reduce the bottleneck of cubing the bread. One machine is capable of creating croutons from pre-sliced bread. Pre-slicing is required as the cubing machine cuts in only two dimensions. The Retail Bakery-Cafe Company produces its own croutons in-house and CFBNJ may be able to coordinate with them for insights on crouton production.

Baking Oven

If production scale increases, CFBNJ may need another oven to handle production. Two options include an additional walk-in oven, similar to the one CFBNJ currently owns, or a baking conveyor belt oven which can produce a more consistent product.

Grinder

A grinder is required for breadcrumb production. CFBNJ can utilize the current grating attachment on its Hobart mixer to produce the desired product, or it may use a commercial grinding machine.

Seasoning

For croutons and bagel chip production, large scale seasoning requires tools to ensure consistency. A kitchen spray bottle can be used to apply oil or melted butter. A spice shaker can be used to apply salt and spices. The seasoning steps may be combined with the baking conveyor belt if CFBNJ decides to customize the production line.

F. Packaging

Resealable packaging was identified by the majority of the survey respondents as the preferred package. Among the resealable packaging alternatives available in the marketplace, selections were narrowed down to fit the project budget, specifications and production scale.

Three types of resealable bags meet the criteria: tin-tie kraft bags, resealable stand-up pouches (saran coated polyester), and resealable stand-up pouches (film foil & polyethylene). Saran coated polyester material is widely used for bakery products as it acts as a strong barrier to oxygen, decreasing spoilage rate and mold growth. Laminated film foil and polyethylene also perform this function well.

Sealing Machines

Various options exist for bag sealing. Manual sealers range from hand held to pedestal sealers with adjustable preset sealing times. Automatic sealers come in a broad range of speeds and volumes.

Labeling Options

In terms of labeling, the team evaluated three options: print the whole label in-house, outsource printing the standard color items of the label followed by printing the ingredients and nutritional facts in-house, and using pre-printed saran bags.

The first option requires a color laser printer and software capable of printing nutritional information. This option provides the flexibility required by variable raw materials. The second option proposes printing the generic portion of the label (color "Grains for Good" logo) through a third party and then printing the variable part of the label in-house (black and white ingredients and nutritional facts). This option also provides the flexibility to handle variable raw materials. The third option is applicable only to the stand-up pouch using saran material. This option would require printing and holding many different versions of the bag/label that would meet the different varieties of bagel chip products.

G. Challenges and Next Steps

The principal challenges to the production of bagel chips include:

- A broad variety of bagels that may be used as inputs.

- Complexity of the recipe required to meet consumers' taste preferences.

- Variable thickness of the product and its effects on baking time and drying consistency.

The proposed next steps include:

- Build up the bill of materials which includes raw materials, seasonings, packaging and labeling supplies.

- Select machinery options to match production scale and requirements including the use of manual vs. automatic machinery and countertop vs. commercial volumes.

- Coordinate logistics with the Retail Bakery-Cafe Company for raw material inputs, routing, and finished product logistics.

4. Financial Model

A. Purpose and Functionality

The goal of the business plan financial model is to provide an objective working spreadsheet model from which financial projections can be made. The model converts user inputted assumptions/facts into summary financial information on 'average week' performance as well as a five-year profit and loss forecast.

The model has been designed to function as an ongoing tool for the project—not for just the delivery of one 'bottom line' number. To that end, the tool has been designed for transparency: as the user inputs values, he/she can also add notes to support those values, e.g. stating assumptions or facts to support the value, providing the project evaluator with insights into the numbers. This feature allows for alternate versions of the model based on different assumptions/facts, including scalability for future increase of scope considerations for the project.

B. Model Layout

The model contains two tabs: 'Inputs' and 'P&L'.

1. Inputs. The 'Inputs' tab contains two sections: the user input area and summary financial information on 'average week' performance.

1a. User input area. The user input area contains 40 line items for input into the model.

Each line item is composed as follows:
- Column A: Input # (for reference)
- Column B: Description of input
- Column C: Space for user entered value
- Column D: Space for user entered assumptions/notes

- Column E: Assessment as to risk involved if assumption is incorrect (sensitivity to effect on project): H = high, M = medium, or L = low

Line items are separated into six categories as follows:
- Materials: concerns project input raw materials and costs to obtain
- Production: concerns converting input raw materials into finished product and costs associated with the process
- Packaging: concerns costs related to product packaging
- Promotion: concerns costs related to merchandising, marketing, and promotion
- Sales: concerns product price and expected sales
- Sales / FC Forecast Factors: concerns variables related to sales volume (including launch uptake curve and seasonality factor) and factor to scale fixed costs

Within these categories, each line item falls under a heading as follows:
- Cap Ex: one-time capital expenditures in quarter 0
- Fixed Costs: expenses that do not depend on product volume
- Variable Costs: expenses that are dependant on product volume
- Input Volume: to determine how much input raw material is available
- Production Volume: to determine how much product can be produced from available input raw material
- Sales Volume: concerns product price and expected sales

1b. Summary Information. The summary information section presents financial metrics for 'average week' business results. 'Average week' is defined by the user via sales volume inputs.

In addition to a 'Total Snapshot' box, summary information is broken down into Materials, Production, Packaging, Promotion, and Sales to directly correlate with user inputs. This design feature helps the evaluator to identify and measure performance, critical success factors, and concerns for each category. For example, the evaluator can see fixed cost and variable cost contributions of each category to total project expenditures.

The 'Expected income per average week' line is highlighted due to its importance—a cursory glance at this line will tell the evaluator if the current assumptions will lead to a project worth considering (i.e. if this line is negative or not at the expectations of the evaluator, the project is most certainly unattractive given the current inputs).

2. P&L. The 'P&L' tab presents a five-year forecasted high-level profit and loss statement as well as some additional project profitability analysis information.

2a. Five-year Forecasted P&L Statement. This section displays expected revenue, revenue growth over previous period, fixed costs, variable costs, earnings, margin percentage, and project-to-date cash flow for each period. Periods are broken down as follows: first year information is shown by month, quarter, and full year; second and third year information is shown by quarter and full year; fourth and fifth year information is shown by full year.

For years two through five, the user can update assumptions for revenue growth over the previous period (for the first year, this information is defined from fields in the 'Inputs' tab). The user can also input an assumed inflation factor to be applied annually to fixed costs beginning in year two.

2b. Additional Project Profitability Information. The lower section of the 'P&L' tab contains other profitability metrics to assist the evaluator in his/her assessment of the project. The user can input the relevant discount rate (i.e. the rate used to calculate the present value of future cash flows) and observe the effect on net present value, or NPV (i.e. the project's net contribution to wealth; the discounted value of future cash flows minus the initial investment). The internal rate of return, or IRR (i.e. the discount rate at which the project would have an NPV of zero), is also reported here.

C. Risk and Uncertainty

When forecasting, one must always consider the distinction between assumptions and facts, as well as the risk and uncertainty inherent in the project and resulting assumptions. As described in column E of the 'Inputs' tab, each line item input has been assessed with the risk involved if assumption is incorrect: high, medium, or low. Risk ratings were assigned based on the sensitivity and uncertainty associated with each input, e.g. a highly sensitive input would materially affect the model's outcome with a slight change to the value and would therefore be assessed as a 'high' risk.

For the model to be relevant, several key areas of 'high' risk in the model must be considered carefully. The 'critical success factors' are as follows:

- Ensuring that production needs are not limited by available input.
- Labor costs are accurately reflected (e.g. is work being done by volunteers or salaried employees?).
- Consideration of any fees or 'pass-through' costs to be reimbursed to the Retail Bakery-Cafe Company.
- Pricing of product.
- Unit sales forecast.

If any of these variables vary from a set of assumptions that shows the project as attractive, the outcome can quickly change the project result. Careful consideration must be given.

D. Spreadsheet File

The business plan financial model has been provided in its Excel spreadsheet form via a CD-ROM that is accompanying this report. Two versions are being provided: (1) with a set of assumptions presenting a 'break-even' breadcrumbs project that was presented during the 'mid-session' presentation on 2 November 2007, and (2) with a set of assumptions presenting a 'break-even' bagel chip project to be discussed during the 'final' presentation on 14 December 2007. Users can modify the presented assumptions and save updated versions of the spreadsheet indefinitely.

5. Conclusions and Recommendations

Using the analysis contained in this report, CFBNJ must carefully consider moving forward with the project. Variability of several high risk inputs makes this a risky undertaking and one which may not be a suitable use of CFBNJ's financial and human capital. If the ultimate decision is to not move forward with the bagel chip product, the possibility of a CRM licensing agreement leveraging the "Grains for Good" brand should be considered as this brand demonstrates considerable strength and matches well with consumers' expectations for CRM campaigns.

Appendix 3C: Final Presentation

Spruce Industries, Inc.

A Feasibility Study on Entering the Consumer Market for "Green" Cleaning Products

Presented by:
the Rider University Student Consulting Team

Industry Outlook

- Modest growth in the demand for cleaning products
- A significant and increasing proportion is expected to come from "green" cleaning supplies
- Some believe the household market for "green" cleaning products will double by 2014

Industry Outlook

- Trend towards "green" cleaning products is increasing rapidly due to 3 factors:
  - Health and environmental benefits they offer
  - As effective if not better than traditional products
  - Competitive pricing

Project Description

The objective of this consulting project is to provide Spruce with strategic business recommendations as it relates to penetrating the consumer market for "green" cleaning products, as follows:

- Private-label Branding
- Product Line
- Process & Feasibility of Obtaining Retail Shelf-Space
- Consumer Website
- Final Recommendations

Consumer Survey- Purpose

- Conducted an online survey to gather consumer perceptions of "green" cleaning products
  - 100 participants
- The survey results provided the team with feedback in 4 major areas of interest
  1.) % of respondents that currently use "green" cleaning products
  2.) The highest utilized cleaning products
  3.) Factors that influence purchase decisions
  4.) Recognition & Influence of "green" certifications on purchase decisions

---

Consumer Survey- Results

- The market for eco-friendly cleaning products currently exists but even more significant are the amount of non-users that could become users in the future
- The three most utilized household cleaning products are: all-surface, bathroom and glass cleaner

Consumer Survey- Results

- Top three factors that influence cleaning product purchase decisions are brand, price and products that have "green"/eco-friendly attributes.
- We would not recommend that Spruce spend the extra money to reflect the Ecologo certification on the cleaning products line labels.

Product line

- Determined by survey results
- Products recommended to carry:
  -All Surface Cleaner
  -Glass Cleaner
  -Restroom Cleaner

Brand Name

- Based on survey results and focus groups
- 10 potential names
- Ultimate decision made by KJP
- ReThink Clean
- Achieves characteristics we were looking for:
  -Simple
  -Effective
  -Powerful
  — Forward-thinking
  — "Green" cleaning

Labeling

- Logo:
  -Tried to include industrial background-Gears
  — "Green" feeling-Earth and Colors
  -Forward thinking-Arrows

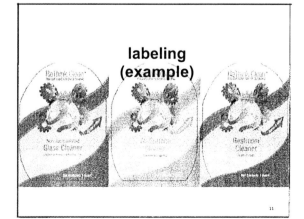

labeling (example)

Process & Feasibility

- 3 different tiers of stores
  -National Stores (Wal-Mart & Target)
  -Regional Stores (Whole Foods & Wegmans)
  -Local-Specialized Stores (Big Bear & Whole Earth Center)

Tier 1

- Wai-Mart & Target
- Largest retailers in the country
- Hard to enter

Wal-Mart

- 4,300 stores in the United States
- Carries 3 different brands of "Green" cleaners
- Prices ranging from $2.77-$2.97
- Online product submission
- Many barriers to entry:
  - Electronic data interchange
  - Lead time requirements
  - Security tagging

Target

- 1,755 stores in the United States
- 3 brands of "green" cleaning products
- Prices from $2.79-$2.99
- Product submission through website
- Production and operation hurdles
- Products containing chemicals cannot be purchased on a regional level

Tier 2

- Whole Foods Market & Wegmans
- Grocery stores
- High emphasis on selling natural and organic products
- Customer base cares about these products

Whole Foods Market

- 300 stores in United States and United Kingdom
- 11stores in New Jersey
- 3 brands of "green" cleaning products
- Prices from $2.79 to $3.99
- Product submission emailed for Northeast and Mid-Atlantic region
- No real interest expressed

Wegmans

- 77 locations in MA, MD, NJ, NY, PA and VA
- 7 locations in New Jersey
- 3 different brands of "green" cleaning products
- Prices from $2.99 to $3.99
- Not much evident information for submission
- Most information for existing vendors

Tier 3

- Big Bear Natural Foods & Whole Earth Center
- Local stores
- Carry only "green," natural and organic products
- Easier access to buyers and owners

Big Bear Natural Foods

- 5 different locations in New Jersey and Pennsylvania
- Different product selection in each store
- 13 different brands of "green" cleaning products
- Prices from $3.99-$8.99
- Buying is done directly by owner
- Interested in:
  - Story of product
  - Look of product
  - Price

Whole Earth Center

- One location in Princeton, New Jersey
- 7 different brands of "green" cleaning products
- Prices from $3.99 to $6.99
- Buying done through general manager
- Interested in:
  - Locally produced
  - Ecologically friendly

Consumer Website Recommendations

- Change name (Potentially Rethink Clean)
- Change log-in location (>visibility)
- Add educational material about "green"/eco-friendly cleaning trends
- Change/remove MSDS location
- Change Resources feature
- Change color scheme (currently dark>brighter colors)

Final Recommendations:
How to Enter the Consumer Market

- Green cleaning product use is growing and will eventually become the consumer standard
- Website sales > Brick and mortar retailers

Final Recommendations:
Who should Spruce Pursue?

- Tier 1-(Wal-Mart and Target)Not feasible at this point
- Tier 2-(Wegmans and Whole Foods) Not feasible at this point
- Tier 3-(Big Bear and Whole Earth) Market test with the Rethink Clean brand

*Identify additional retailers between Tier 2 & Tier 3 (Shop & Bag NJ-9, PA-18)

Appendix 3D: "Thank You" Letter

Date
Client Name
Business Name
Address
City, State Zip

Dear (Client's Name):

It has been a pleasure to work with you in an analysis of your firm. Your cooperation, patience, and enthusiasm made our job much easier and contributed to our learning. We feel you have given us a great opportunity to use our formal education in a real-world application.

Our report makes recommendations based upon your input and our analysis. We hope that the implementation of these recommendations will benefit your company.

This report should not be interpreted as the official position of the (school) or its staff. Instead, the report contains the views and opinions of the student team based upon our discussions, observations, investigations, and analysis of both internal and external business conditions relative to your firm's operations.

Any questions or comments you may have should be directed to the student team leader (before graduation on *(date and phone number)*) or to our instructor, (_____). Again, thank you.

Sincerely,

Student Team Member   Student Team Member

Student Team Member   Student Team Member

Appendix 3E: Sample Syllabus

CONSULTING FOR NEW AND SMALL BUSINESSES   (MBA class)

Professor:

Required Materials: Textbook- The Experiential Student Team Consulting Process; 4th edition, Cook, Belliveau, & Campbell;   Blackboard URL:

Course Objectives:

This course provides "experience-based" learning to students through the use of student teams to assist area small businesses/organizations. These small firms/organizations could have a wide variety of needs ranging from market research, business planning, operational issues, etc.

Statistics from the US Census Department show that over 98% of all firms employ less than 500 people and these same firms employ over 55% of the total private sector workforce. If you seek employment in smaller-sized firms, chose consulting as a career path, or chose to start your own firm or join a family business, this type of experience will be invaluable.

In addition, the course is designed to:

1) provide students with opportunities to assist small businesses/organizations (clients);

2) allow students to utilize their businesses skills in an experiential learning environment;

3) duplicate the business consulting process; and,

4) enhance the school's presence in the community.

Method of Evaluation:

Students will be evaluated primarily on the quality of the solution that they will have proposed to meet a client's needs. Student teams will first be matched to a client. The teams will develop a Letter of Engagement (LOE) that will be agreed to by the client, the students, and myself.

Students will be required to file progress reports (1 per team) of their activities and contacts with the clients, which will be reviewed every 2 weeks. This course uses the Blackboard® program on the Rider web site to provide information/documentation to students. These reports, client feedback, the peer evaluation, and my judgment of your ability to operate in a professional manner will constitute 30% of your grade.

As the project develops, students will turn in a briefing paper, the Letter of Engagement, and 2 sections from the project (see deadline sheet/web site for times). The briefing paper and the 2 sections will each constitute 10% of your grade, and the LOE will constitute 5%. The final deliverable will be a completed project/presentation, based on the team's LOE.

The course would initially meet during its scheduled time for the first week to develop teams and chose projects. After that, teams would meet bi-weekly with the professor to review their progress. Teams will be expected to document 3-5 hours weekly of project research when the class is not meeting. The following breakdown represents the grading:

Briefing paper on industry	10%
Homework sections of project	20%
Letter of Engagement	5%
Reports/evaluations/participation	30%
Completed project/presentation	35%
Total	100%

Group Dynamics:

The entire course is structured for student teams to work outside of the classroom and help small firms/organizations. The team is an essential part of this process. 70% of your grade is based on the efforts of your team so the key is to develop good synergy. I want each team to work well and I may be conducting team building exercises with the teams as the semester progresses. Let's work together to help out the client.

Final Grade: The following is the letter grade you will receive when the various components are added up:

Grade	Point Total
A	94 or more
A-	89-93
B+	86-88
B	81-85
B-	78-80
C+	74-77
C	70-73
C-	67-69
F	67 or less

Additional Deadlines and Comments:

1) Briefing paper on Industry- This paper should have two parts:
    a) Industry trends in the particular business you are working with.
    b) Competition for the particular firm you are working with (top 3-4).

2) Project outline- This is due on _____. It should represent the format of the final report and will serve as the table of contents.

3) Two sections of the final report- Content will vary by team but they are due on __ and __

4) Completed project/presentation- This is the largest part of the courseYou will make a presentation to the company at Rider on or before __. You will turn a final version of the project in to me by ___. I will review that and grade it and then return it to you so you can make whatever changes are needed before your presentation to the client.

5) Photo shoot When the clients are brought into Rider for the final presentations, the firms and the student teams will have their picture taken.

SAMPLE CASE STUDY PROCESS

Week 1:
-Project teams assigned.
-Review client's project request
-Teams sign "Confidentiality Agreement"
-Read text up to appendices
-Post meeting minutes in Blackboard
-Complete Journal assignment 1

Week 1-2:
-Develop an agenda for future meeting with client
-Review Possible Questions for Analysis
-Maintain "Activity Log"
-Fill out "Progress Report"
-Post meeting minutes in Blackboard
-Schedule and conduct initial client meeting to:
        -Tour facility and meet key staff
        -Leave copy of "Confidentiality Agreement
        -Leave copy of Company Contact Sheet

Week 3:
-Maintain "Activity Log"
-Fill out "Progress Report"
-Meet with Dr. Cook at assigned times
-Post meeting minutes in Blackboard
- Create Letter of Engagement

Weeks 4-10:
-Reference textbook sections as needed
-Deliver Letter of Engagement
-Ensure that letter of Engagement is returned
-Work on your project
-Contact client as needed
-Prepare interim report if needed
-Ongoing presentation and final report preparation
-Maintain "Activity Log"
-Fill out "Progress Reports"
-Meet with Dr. Cook at assigned times
-Post meeting minutes in Blackboard
- Complete Journal assignment 2 (about week 7)

Weeks 11 & 12:
-Complete Final Report
-Post meeting minutes in Blackboard
-Conduct presentation with client at Rider to:
       Present and discuss findings
       Leave a copy of report with thank you letter
       Conduct photo shoot

Week 13:
- Submit peer evaluation and completed activity log to Dr. Cook
- Complete Journal Assignment 3

Appendix 3E: Sample Syllabus

TEAM CONSULTING
Professor: Office Hours: By Appointment

Required text: The Experiential Student Team Consulting Process, 4th edition Cook, Belliveau & Campbell

Other reading materials: To be distributed electronically or in class.

Course Objectives

This is a required, capstone course that presents students with an experiential learning opportunity that's both integrative and interfunctional. The clinical rather than classroom approach uses fee-based consulting engagements to help students:

(1) Gain understanding from the practical, field application of the knowledge gained from classrooms and textbooks.
(2) Develop skills to meet the integrative demands of collaborative, multi-discipline problem solving.

Teamwork is a major part of this experiential learning course as students improve project management capabilities and communications skills, both verbal and written.

Learning Outcomes

Upon completion of this course, students will have demonstrated an understanding of:

(1) The steps necessary to develop and facilitate a project plan.
(2) The group collaborative process in decision making and project performance.
(3) How to recognize and conceptualize a complex issue into a clearly written summary.

Written Assignments

The major written assignments are:

(1) Letter of Engagement (LOE) -- Prepared in collaboration with client and completed at Week #4.

(2) Interim Reports -- As specified in the LOE.

(3) Final Report -- Based on analysis of primary and secondary research and delivered to client at project end in the form established in the LOE.

(4) Final Presentation -- Usually an executive summary of the final report, rehearsed at next to last week and presented at last week.

In addition, teams are required to submit weekly activity reports and weekly timesheets to their Advisor.

Grading Criteria

(1) Anonymous Peer Evaluations	25%
(2) Client Team Evaluation	25%
(3) Advisor's Team Grade	25%
(4) Advisor's Individual Grade	25%

COURSE OUTLINE

<u>Phase 1</u>

Week 1	1) Course Introduction 2) Go over syllabus and course outline 3) Form and organize teams 4) Begin secondary research on client
Week 2	1) Prepare for first meeting with client 2) Meet with client 3) Begin LOE process with client
Week 3	1) LOE draft, revised in class 2) Send LOE to client for review and comment 3) Copy of LOE to Director before signing
Week 4	1) LOE finalized and signed 2) Project tasks assigned to team

<u>Phase 2</u>

Weeks 5-8	1) Research and analysis 2) On-going development of report
Week 9	1) Complete research and preliminary analysis 2) Continue development of report.

<u>Phase 3</u>

Week 10	1) Draft final report for internal review and gap assessment
Week 11	1) Second draft of final report 2) First draft of final presentation
Week 12	1) Third draft of final report 2) Second draft of final presentation
Week 13	1) Dry run final presentation

Week 14   1) Final presentation to client

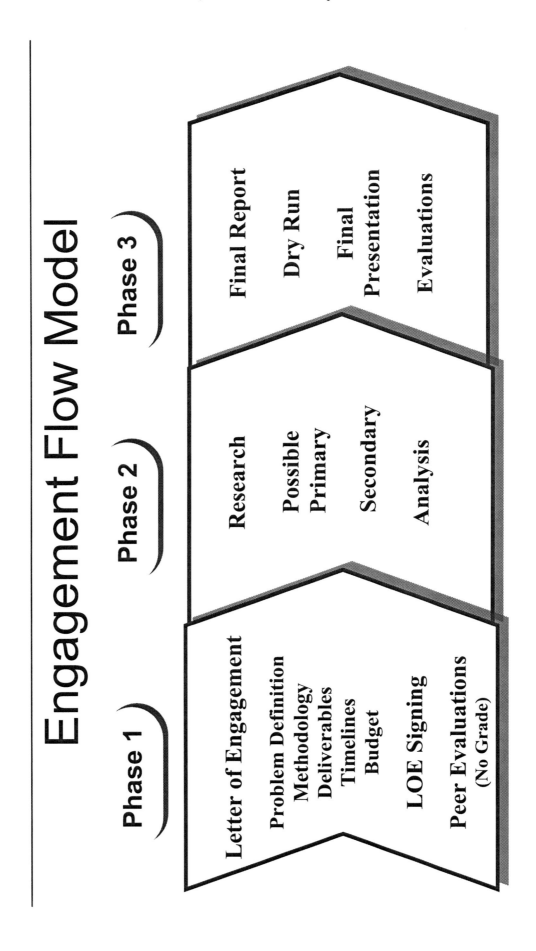

Engagement Flow Model

Phase 1

Letter of Engagement

Problem Definition
Methodology
Deliverables
Timelines
Budget

LOE Signing

Peer Evaluations
(No Grade)

Phase 2

Research

Possible
Primary

Secondary

Analysis

Phase 3

Final Report

Dry Run

Final
Presentation

Evaluations

Endnotes:

[i] Rutgers Business School MBA Team Consulting Program Brochure, Rutgers, The State University of New Jersey. http://business.rutgers.edu

[ii] Matthews, Charles, 1998. "The Small Business Institute Program: High Impact Entrepreneurship Education", Journal of Small Business Strategy, 9(2):14-22.

[iii] Kenworthy-U'ren, A. L. (2008). A decade of service-learning: A review of the field ten years after JOBE's seminal special issue. *Journal of Business Ethics*, 81(4), 811–822.

[iv] Maskulka, T. A., Stout, D. E., & Massad, V. J. (2011). Using and assessing an experiential learning project in a retail marketing course. *Journal of Instructional Pedagogies*, 6, 1–20.

[v] Kickul, J., Griffiths, M., & Bacq, S. (2010). The boundary-less classroom: Extending social innovation and impact learning to the field. Journal of Small Business and Enterprise Development, 17(4), 652–663.

[vi] Brownell, J., & Jameson, D. A. (2004). Problem-based learning in graduate management education: An integrative model and interdisciplinary application. Journal of Management Education, 28(5), 558–577.

[vii] Peterson, T. O. (2004). So you're thinking of trying problem-based learning?: Three critical success factors for implementation. *Journal of Management Education*, 28(5), 630–647. (P. 630?)

[viii] Brownell, J., & Jameson, D. A. (2004). Problem-based learning in graduate management education: An integrative model and interdisciplinary application. Journal of Management Education, 28(5), 558–577.

[ix] Ibid.

[x] Godfrey, P. C., Illes, L. M., & Berry, G. R. (2005). Creating Breadth in Business Education Through Service-Learning. *Academy Of Management Learning & Education*, 4(3), 309-323. (P. 309?)

[xi] Ibid.

[xii] Brownell, J., & Jameson, D. A. (2004). Problem-based learning in graduate management education: An integrative model and interdisciplinary application. Journal of Management Education, 28(5), 558–577. Page#?

[xiii] Ibid. Page#?

[xiv] Ibid.

[xv] Ibid. P. 565

[xvi] Warters, W. (2000). Conflict Resolution Tools and Tips for Students. Retrieved June 5,2003 from http://www.campus-adr.org/Student_Center/tips_student.html, p.6.

[xvii] Gill, T., Heermans, K., & Herath, R. (1998). Puzzled about teams, a handbook. Retrieved June 5, 2003 from http://www.inov8.psu.edu/toolbox/PuzzledAboutTeams.pdf, p.6

[xviii] Ibid.

xix Ibid..

xx Lyons, B. (2003). Group diseases in the science classroom: A reference guide to symptoms and treatments. Retrieved June 5, 2003 from http://www2.canisius.edu/~morriss/bio201/groups.html.

xxi Ibid.

xxii Gill, T., Heermans, K., & Herath, R. (1998). Puzzled about teams, a handbook. Retrieved June 5, 2003 from http://www.inov8.psu.edu/toolbox/PuzzledAboutTeams.pdf.

xxiii Ibid.

xxiv Ibid.

xxv Pearce, J. A. II, & Robinson, R.B. Jr. (1994). Strategic Management: Formulation, Implementation, and Control. (5th edition). Burr Rider, IL:Irwin.

xxvi Porter, M. E. (1998). Competitive Strategy: Techniques For Analyzing Industries and Competitors. New York: Free Press.

xxvii Small Business Institute® (1997). Small Business Institute® Student Consulting Manual. Available from the Small Business Institute®, www.smallbusinessinstitute.org.

xxviii Peterson, T. O. (2004). So you're thinking of trying problem-based learning?: Three critical success factors for implementation. Journal of Management Education, 28(5), 630–647.

xxix www.servicelearning.org, (n.d.). Retrieved April 3, 2012.

xxx Eyler, J. & Giles, D. E. (1999). Where's the Learning in Service-learning?. San Francisco: Jossey Bass.

xxxi What is Service Learning? (n.d.) Retrieved April 12, 2012 from emedia.leeward.hawaii.edu/servicelearning/what_is.htm.

xxxii Kenworthy-U'ren, A. L. (2008). A decade of service-learning: A review of the field ten years after JOBE's seminal special issue. Journal of Business Ethics, 81(4), 811–822.

xxxiii Kenworthy-U'ren, A. L. (2000) Management Students as Consultants: A Strategy for Service-Learning in Management Education. Pp. 55-68 in Godfrey, P. & Grasso, E. (Eds)'s Working for the Common Good: Concepts and Models for Service-Learning in Management. Washington, D.C.: AAHE.org

xxxiv Hartman, L., & Werhane, P. (2009). A Modular Approach to Business Ethics Integration: At the Intersection of the Stand-Alone and the Integrated Approaches. Journal Of Business Ethics, 90, 295-300.

xxxv Dumas, C. (2002). Community-Based Service-Learning: Does It Have a Role in Management Education? International Journal of Value-Based Management, 15 (3), 249-264.

xxxvi Kenworthy-U'ren, A. L. (2008). A decade of service-learning: A review of the field ten years after JOBE's seminal special issue. Journal of Business Ethics, 81(4), 811–822.

xxxvii Kenworthy-U'ren, A. L. (2000) Management Students as Consultants: A Strategy for Service-Learning in Management Education. Pp. 55-68 in Godfrey, P. & Grasso, E. (Eds)'s Working for the Common Good: Concepts and Models for Service-Learning in Management. Washington, D.C.: AAHE.org [xxxviii] Kolenko, T. A., Porter, G., Wheatley, W., & Colby, M. (1996). A critique of service-learning projects in management education: Pedagogical foundations, barriers, and guidelines. *Journal of Business Ethics*, 15(1), 133.

[xxxix] Brownell, J., & Jameson, D. A. (2004). Problem-based learning in graduate management education: An integrative model and interdisciplinary application. Journal of Management Education, 28(5), 558–577.

[xl] Maskulka, T. A., Stout, D. E., & Massad, V. J. (2011). Using and assessing an experiential learning project in a retail marketing course. *Journal of Instructional Pedagogies*, 6, 1–20.

[xli] Ames, Michael, D. (2006). "AACSB international advocacy of experiential learning and assurance of learning-boom or bust for SBI student consulting." In L. Tombs, (ed), USASBE/SBI 2006 Joint Conference Proceedings, January 12-15, 2006, Tucson, AZ.

[xlii] Maskulka, T. A., Stout, D. E., & Massad, V. J. (2011). Using and assessing an experiential learning project in a retail marketing course. *Journal of Instructional Pedagogies*, 6, 1–20.

INDEX

A
AACSB, 38
Accomplish level, 40
Activity logs, 16
Assessment, See evaluation
Assurance of learning, 38

B
Baseline measure of knowledge, 39

C
CI area, 7, 8
CIT area, 7, 8
Client phase (Process Flow Model), 18, 19
    client issues, 18,
    competition comparison, 19, 20
    initial meeting, 22, 23
    preliminary industry analysis, 18
    problem identification, 21, 22
Clients
    acquisition (Process Flow Model), 12
    client's team evaluations, 32
    contacts, 14
    environment, 18
    instructor's individual evaluations, 33
    instructor's team evaluations, 33
    lack of responsiveness, 22
    LOE
        problem definition, 23
        project communication, 27
        project management, 26
    as part of student team consulting model, 7
Communication
    between team members, 14
Competition comparison, 19, 20
Compromise, 14
Confidentiality, 10
Conflict resolution, 14
    client issues, 18
    reasons for conflicts, 15-16
Conflicts of interest, 10
Consulting
    student team consulting, 3, 4